# PERSONALLY ASSURED DESTRUCTION

Understand and End Self-Sabotage to Stop
Overthinking, Increase Your Productivity and
Overcome Self-defeating Behaviors

## DAMIEN BLAKE

## Self-Sabotage - A Weapon of Mass Destruction

*"Most of us have two lives. The life we live and the unlived life within us. Between the two stands resistance."* - Academy of Ideas (2018).

Why do we ruin the things we want the most out of life? Why do we deny ourselves the life that we always wanted to live? Because it's a self-defense mechanism! It can affect pretty much every part of our lives - professional, romantic, social, financial, etc. Anything good in our lives CAN be sabotaged, and sometimes we do not even know we are doing precisely that.

Have you ever had one of those days where you feel that you just simply *can't*? You start off snoozing through four alarm clocks and arriving late at work just casts a foreboding shadow on the rest of your day. You have? Well good! We've at least established that you are human! But have you ever found yourself feeling stuck in neutral? That place where you feel you can't achieve anything, no matter how hard you try?

If you find yourself in such a negative frame of mind nearly every day, then my friend, you might be sabotaging yourself into having that bad day. Like in Tom Cruise's *Edge of Tomorrow*—only this time, there is no tomorrow to look forward to, "because it will only be the same as today." You know that "same shit different day" mentality and attitude towards life. Many people mistake self-sabotage for bad luck or negative cataclysm - they will often even use phrases like "knowing my luck, this is never gonna work," "I just have a really bad fortune," etc.

*How many of us don't currently live the life that we envisioned for ourselves?*— The one we genuinely want, crave, and deserve? Have you ever found yourself tirelessly working towards a certain goal but then crashing and burning spectacularly? All due to your constant overthinking, overanalyzing, or making stupid mistakes?

As if that wasn't enough, you then feel the need to punish yourself for "underperforming" and spend hours beating yourself up over things that are often not even in your control. Again, the saying definitely rings true - *"we are all responsible for our own shit."* However, that critical inner voice can be a bit of a bastard—all too often; it is your own worst enemy instead of being your cheerleader. Why? Because you allow it to be this way!

By allowing that inner self-critic to dictate your life, you may have been missing out on all of the beautiful opportunities that have come your way. This might very well be the reason why, despite your best efforts, you come up very short in acing your goals.

The great news that I simply *have* to share with you is that even if you're finding yourself in the deepest depths of despair—there is hope, and I am definitely in your corner on this! In this book, not only will you find detailed advice on how to overcome it, but also two true stories from self-saboteurs who agreed to share their experience in the hopes of helping others.

Even if you are so immersed in feeling sorry for yourself, you should know that this is a much more common occurrence than you think. So often, we tend to hit that self-destruction button of auto-sabotage without even knowing. Like butt dialing a random contact when you forgot to lock your phone - you don't know you're doing it, but it certainly does not make it any less real.

Have you ever felt and known that you are procrastinating and resisting change? And at the end of the day, you look at your daily to-do list and then think that you've achieved diddly squat? Just to race home, fall into a routine, drag your ass out of bed the following day... rinse and repeat...you get my drift? We will unpack the resistance and best ways to deal with it in detail in further chapters.

As uncomfortable as it may sound, your procrastination is the very reason why your productivity levels are low or even worse—are utterly non-existent at the moment. In this book, I aim to help you come to terms with and understand your auto-sabotage tendencies and provide you with a path to getting back on track with your career, relationships, and pretty much every other part of your life! That beautiful zen state of being that makes you go *ahhhh* and close your eyes in the pleasure of enjoying-the-moment-kinda-place! You deserve to be happy in every sense of the word.

Get ready for a blueprint that can give you a different perspective on life and give you the platform for a complete lifestyle overhaul. We can achieve it by identifying the tendencies and issues that are hampering you from living your best life and becoming versed with practical strategies to combat them!

You can also expect to discover a range of options and techniques to be unpacked in our journey together to find your life's design that works for YOU!

# What is Self-Sabotage? Am I Doing it?

*"Self-sabotage is when we say we want something and then go about making sure that it doesn't happen."* – Liggett (n.d.)

## The Calling

It is a tale that is as old as time. As humans, at times, we seem to have an inner calling to rise to the occasion. For example, you might turn up late for work constantly, but at some point, you might feel a nagging *pull*–an *inclination*, if you will to tell yourself actually to start getting up earlier and *carpe diem* the day! Sometimes it is triggered by a specific event (like getting a warning from your boss), and sometimes it is purely our dissatisfaction with our current identity of self (identity of an unpunctual person in this example) - a deep subconscious frustration with our own choices. Sadly, very often, our resolve to change fleets quickly, and we then might just decide that there is no point trying anyway.

.   .   .

In 1988 researchers Norcross and Vangarelli conducted an experiment attempting to measure the rates of people that will actually stick to the goals they set out to achieve after having this moment of need for change. They chose a group of people who had made New Year's resolutions to try and get some answers. 77% have given up after maintaining their pledges for one week or less. However, it came as a real surprise that out of the remaining 23% of the study, 19% of total participants were still following their new pattern of behavior two years later. Therefore, only 4% of participants lasted somewhere between a week and two years. (Changing Habits, 2019).

What does this mean, you may ask? Well, firstly, we could make an assumption (with some reservations, of course) that those who kept going, kept pushing for just another day, have actually managed to go significantly longer or even permanently implement the change. However, the 77% (more than three out of four participants) giving up within the first week is shocking! This inner calling requires us to stand up, grow, and make advancement to the next level – one in which we are summoned to lead a more fulfilling life, and one that holds invaluable benefits for us, should we accept this challenge! So why do the vast majority of us choose to go back to the old habits that we were so eager to change less than a week ago?

***Damien's Tip:*** *Experts advise that those who are focusing on only one aspect at a time (e.g., becoming more punctual) are significantly more successful at maintaining the changes than those who picked multiple aspects to change (e.g., eat healthier, AND exercise more, AND save 20% of monthly salary). It would appear that over-*

*whelming yourself with everything at once may not be the best idea. Instead, start with one change at a time and move on to the next one when the previous one is implemented fully.*

This type of inner calling often comes to us when we are not in a good space mentally, physically, or otherwise. But, unfortunately, we tend to ignore the calling because we are trapped in our comfort zone. We are sometimes aware of the fact that good things happen outside of our comfort bubble, but we have an innate *want* to remain in this "safe space." And therefore, once life-changing opportunities come knocking, we almost always feel unprepared and not ready to take them on!

Yet, this is when this calling is at its most effective! Each time this happens, you are standing in front of two doors:

- **Door number 1:** Embrace it and work to change some aspect of your life, or
- **Door number 2:** Continue on the current path of dormant life and get carried by the current all the deeper into its choking abyss.

At first, opening door number one seems like the quickest way out of the quicksand and back onto stable ground (and in most cases, it probably is). Sadly, in most of these situations, we cannot forge ahead and handle these changes as they come—primarily due to all sorts of self-sabotaging tendencies that we have. Accepting the change is equal to stepping out far outside of the comfort zone. Then all of our senses are screaming– fueling our over-thinking, second thoughts, fear of failure, etc. – almost demanding we go back to that negative perception. At the very least, we think that it is a comfortable, well-charted territory of old habits. The result is us going back to the foyer and shamefully opening door number two again– because it is *easier* and it is *familiar* even though we know it will come back to bite us in the butt again and again! Ever heard the saying "old habits, die hard"? They truly do.

When we make a serious attempt and step out far outside the comfort zone, it does not come gently. Instead, it is a booming and thunderous voice of our inner critic and our fears that demands from us to heed its expectations–like a bolt of lightning out of an African sky against an iron-rich mountain biosphere! As a result, most people gasp with "I was not ready for this yet," –creating themselves an excuse to abandon their new path.

Make no mistake, we still want to improve ourselves by growing, and the vast majority of the population want to be millionaires, gain fame or leave a mark in history in some other way. And we all have the potential to do so –we are simply not willing and disciplined enough to fight for it and navigate through the sometimes tumultuous turns of change. We want the gains, but without the pain. We want the fruits without putting in the hard labor first. Our deter-mination waivers just a little too quickly, especially when so-called defense mechanisms seem to be working against us in these situations.

## What is Self-Sabotage?

The person sabotaging themselves, also referred to as a saboteur is more often than not engaged in a series of events where they deliberately and directly involve themselves in their downfall!

It is a word that you might've heard *again and again* by now, but getting a firm grasp on what that means is no easy feat. Why? Because many saboteurs don't even know or refuse to accept that they are self-sabotaging. Sometimes it is easier to live in your self-created illusions.

Some people use this word to judge other people, especially those they perceive as weak or lazy. Other individuals casually use it as a term to sound smart. Still, many of them have no idea what they are talking about and often converse about it as if it is meaningless and feel pretty indifferent about it.

As the word says, self-sabotage is when your destructive behavior is directed at yourself. In the beginning, you might not even notice or know that this is happening to you. But when your own bad habits become so destructive that they are constantly diminishing your best efforts at self-improvement, in the psychological hemisphere, it can be categorized as a form of self-harm (Self-sabotage, n.d.).

Self-sabotage has an adverse impact on your daily life and does not only transcend into longer-term goals only. For example, it can stop you from making choices such as eating healthy, quitting smoking, or even just getting a decent night's sleep. So self-sabotage will attack you, no matter how big or mundane a form it might manifest itself. I have mentioned this already, but remember - this is often a self-defense mechanism, and your mind thinks it is doing you a favor.

Allowing self-sabotage to consume your life will set you up for definitive failure—guaranteed, no questions asked! But, as twisted as it sounds, if you've created this alternate reality in your mind that you are doomed to failure, and it happens, you might even get a sense of satisfaction from it because "I told you so" and because "I knew it."

Medical professionals such as psychologists and psychiatrists have found that when most of their patients sit on their couch for their weekly session, the individual's failures are almost presented as prizes. As if this is the only thing they have achieved and the only thing that they were right about. Worst of all, it appears to the saboteur that this is the only facet of their lives where they feel they are in the driving seat and in control, as it is much easier to make yourself fail than to make yourself succeed. (MedCircle, 2021).

## Where Does Self-Sabotaging Behavior Come From?

We've already discussed some of the ways in which self-sabotage can present itself. But, just like the plethora of ways it can happen, it is also imperative to know that there can be just as many reasons behind it taking root and developing over time.

Before we proceed further, I have to ingrain in your mind that there is often not only one particular reason why people self-sabotage. If you find yourself in a situation where you seek a straightforward answer, it implies that you don't fully grasp the concept and what it will take to conquer it! Our minds are complex, and in most cases, there will be many reasons and past experiences that have fortified your comfort zone with self-sabotaging defenses.

## How do I Know If I am Self-Sabotaging?

If you aren't even sure if you are a self-sabotager, then ask yourself the following questions:

- Do you find yourself overthinking and overanalyzing everything you do, to the point where you make crappy decisions with adverse outcomes because you don't trust your own judgment and inner gut?
- Does your inner voice constantly criticize you and see the worst in every situation you encounter—much to your regret later—but then it's too late? Then it starts all damn over again and gives you a lashing of the non-sexy kind?
- Have you ever felt that you sadly possess an unfortunate natural inclination to think that the world is against you?
- Do you feel like you can't form lasting friendships and relationships because you see

7

things in other people that you hate, making you bitter towards them?

- Has anyone ever told you that you tend to pick fights? As a result, making you feel underappreciated, unvalued, and that your opinion doesn't matter, even though this was not your intention at all?
- Do you suffer from low self-esteem and just hate your life or the melancholy you find yourself in?
- Have you ever felt anxious and stressed because you have this big goal to achieve, but then the negative cycle of lambasting yourself continues, making you feel more angry and frustrated with yourself?

If you have answered yes, to any of the above questions, you likely have some tendencies of behavior that may be worth trying to gain a deeper understanding of.

## 21 Real-Life Examples Of Self-Sabotage Mechanisms

It is completely natural for any person to engage in a form of self-sabotage at some point in their life. In some instances, it can exhibit itself in only a moderate or casual form, whereby it does not frequently occur, resulting in minor consequences. However, it comes in a more severe and chronic form for other individuals and impacts their entire livelihood.

Self-sabotage is often initiated by constant negative self-talk or thoughts that bring your worth and value into question.

Of course, we've all gone through these motions, and some more than others (ask me, I know), but some of us are more predisposed to getting hooked on this negative type of behavior than others.

We are all different, and it can sometimes be hard to come to terms that we are, in fact, harming ourselves. Most people immediately react with "I would never!". However, self-awareness is becoming a super-power in today's modern society. When some crucial realizations occur, do not ignore the signs or that gut feeling you have. Shutting down those lightbulb moments will only empower your self-sabotage to instill a sense of worthlessness in you (which I assure you, you aren't worthless) and provide validation in your mind for justifying the negative thoughts and feelings you encounter.

Self-sabotage has many *different* hats. Please read the rest of the chapter with your mind open and try to see if these behaviors align with any patterns in your own life. Some of the most commonly found forms of self-sabotage are:

**1. Chronic Lateness**. When individuals constantly arrive late for everything, this might very well be a sign that they are sabotaging themselves. Some people do this because they have social anxiety and prefer not to "people" too much at events.

However, what they may not realize at this point is that people don't trust them and will also likely not be interested in forming any sort of meaningful connection with them in the long run. Mostly due to a perceived lack of respect. It also affects their personal brand negatively to an extent where it becomes tough to make a recovery. When everyone always expects that person to be late and brands them as "that person" - always last to arrive, it only reinforces the person's belief that they are indeed that person, encouraging the negative pattern.

**2. Commitment and Intimacy Issues.** Others might be in perfectly happy relationships and then find themselves doing anything and everything to derail that happy relationship. In most cases, these saboteurs are afraid of getting hurt and have difficulty navigating the waters of emotional vulnerability.

They will instead put these relationships and friendships up as collateral damage, and when it doesn't work in their favor, they actually experience some sort of anxiety relief. For instance, a person with intimacy issues will often alter their behavior as intimacy gets more intense. They potentially fear abandonment and, therefore, will pull back to protect themselves and will also likely mistreat their partner to reduce the level of intimacy. Other common denominators are: unreasonable jealousy, attempts to control the life of their partner, sleeping with other people, overly criticizing the partner, etc.

**3. Procrastination.** This probably has to be the most common universal self-sabotage tendency of all! Because it implies that we know we put off doing something that does need to happen at some point in time or conveniently "for-get" to do something.

Just stopping for no reason, but I mean to a complete halt. You've got all the tools, resources, and skills to complete the project; you know you need to get it done for your own good, but the will to execute has expired, or you choose to do the things that are more instantly gratifying. In some cases, we abandon the critical, life-changing tasks. This is where negative mindset or *scarcity mentality* often plays a huge part - "I won't bother finishing that cover letter - I'm not going to get that job anyway." So naturally, the self-fulfilling prophecy phenomenon occurs. You don't finish the letter as you don't think you are good enough for the job or don't think you stand a chance, and it turns out to be true as with no application or unfinished documents, the chances of landing that job are significantly reduced. Self-sabotage is right in front of us!

**4. Waiting Until Last Minute Dot Com.** Procrastina-tion and putting off getting things done generally are sometimes a result of lethargy, boredom, or even just simply feeling overwhelmed. But, again, it is entirely normal to put something off from time to time because you don't feel like it. But feeling *meh*! constantly is a severe cause for concern and can have dire consequences if not actioned quickly. "I can start it tomorrow or next week" is a hazardous form of self-sabotage! In addition, because you might feel bored or not in the mood to do something constantly, you feel more stressed or depressed because you've left something until the last minute and you are now feeling overwhelmed.

. . .

**5. Stress-eating.** Some people completely fast when they self-sabotage, and others turn to food as a crutch. When this saboteur constantly consumes food, it gives them a short-lived sense of instant gratification where they feel good about themselves. It also serves to forget the pain and the inevitable that needs to be dealt with.

However, they are fully aware that by doing so, they are impacting their health negatively and that there will be consequences to face eventually as this is not conducive behavior. For example, when you get home from a "long, boring and stressful day at work," the last thing you might feel like doing is cooking. So what do you do - ordering online is your new norm. This way, you don't have to cook or even think of something healthier to eat as it requires too much effort on your part. Someone else cooks for you, so you can just pour over the Netflix menu and binge-watch your favorite shows. Being stuck in a job where you constantly feel uninspired is just an example but also a widespread occurrence–it pours fuel into the fire of all sorts of mental and physical health issues. It is easy to use it as a constant "get out of jail" card to justify all kinds of bad decisions and choices.

**6. Substance Abuse.** There is nothing wrong with having a cold brewski every now and again, but it becomes a problem when it turns into a habit that takes you away from your responsibilities. Drug and alcohol abuse will always interfere with your goals at hand. For example - you are going to the local bar every night, knowing that there are issues in your intimate relationship to resolve. Let's face it, "I am not in the mood for her nagging tonight," and just like that, you have justified it to yourself, taking yourself away from your responsibility towards your marriage.

Another classic example might be a student with a great affinity to become one of the best veterinary surgeons. But instead of studying the large volume of material in preparation for your exams, "I don't feel like studying, and I always feel good after having a few drinks; it helps me to cope with the pressure."

***Damien's tip***: *It is sometimes tough to go "cold turkey" if drugs/alcohol has become a part of your daily rituals. E.g., a friend of mine had a habit of smoking joints late at night after a stressful day at work. He said that the calming effects of cannabis combined with the sounds of the city quieting down were easing all the effects of stress and helping him sleep.*

*However, over time he started smoking every day regardless of the stress levels. After becoming self-aware that it was getting out of hand, he started using that smoke as a way of self-rewarding. He created a rule for himself to only smoke at night if he feels he has been very productive during the day. Thus, he used his addiction to become much more productive (working for that reward). Over time, with constantly increasing productivity, the stress levels have reduced (as he got all things on the to-do list done most of the time) it reduced the need for relieving the stress with smoking. The reduced amount of drug intake has allowed him to manage and conquer the addiction completely.*

. . .

*In my book "Modern Alpha Male Mindset Strategies," I have presented the Incremental Model for Success concept. If you cannot make instant changes and you know from experience, you will just bounce back—take an incremental change approach and implement minor changes to slowly ease out of whatever habit you are trying to change. Some refer to it as "1% better every day" or "one day at a time." Alternatively, you can also try to reduce temptations by removing them from your house (whether it's alcohol, junk food, or anything else you would be consuming)—you're much less likely to reach for the bottle if there is no bottle to reach for*

**7. Constant Self-Criticism.** If you are constantly criticizing yourself, it is possible that you cannot forgive yourself for the mistakes you've made previously. You are not able to just let it go - instead, you replay it over and over in your mind. Sound all too familiar? Then you might be harming yourself in your quest for perfection. When you strive to always be perfect in everything you do, the truth is that you will never be satisfied. Having perfection as your end goal in life is unrealistic, to say the least!

When you are afraid of making any form of mistake, you paralyze yourself from making any productive progress forward in the right direction. This also has a highly negative impact on your overall mental health because you will always feel like the things in your life are not good enough, like your performance is not good enough, etc. For example, you messed up the report's figures once because you went against your better judgment of double-checking the information. It was a small typo, but you are so afraid of messing up again that you are constantly trying to overcompensate because you don't want to make the same mistake again. There is a big difference between learning from a mistake and creating a fear within you of repeating the error.

**8. Always Pointing Out the Negative.** Would you say that you are an individual that analyzes the shit out of every situation and picks it apart until you are satisfied that there are no more flaws to be found? Like the opposite of looking for a silver lining. Does it come as a surprise to you when things do go your way "for a change"?

If so, this negative mindset might have resulted in a lack of meaningful and lasting relationships in your life. After all, you are constantly pessimistic and therefore do not expect these relationships to end well. Furthermore, people who are always whining and complaining about life can also be seen as sort of energetic vampires. It is exhausting to be around people who constantly nag, never see the beauty of life around them, and see only a negative outcome in every situation. So again, pessimism sabotages your ideals, dreams, relationships, and even your health in general.

In relation to health matters, studies have shown that persons that self-identify as a pessimist are 2,2 times more likely to succumb to coronary cardiac diseases. (Pessimism associated with risk of death from coronary heart disease, 2016).

**9. Inability to Get Organized.** Is living in disarray perhaps your sense of "normal"? This in itself is a severe form of auto-sabotage and will see factors such as your self-esteem declining (more on this in a later chapter), losing sight of things that you actually *need,* and the things that you *want.*

When you repeatedly feel like you are not in control, you are susceptible to illnesses and conditions such as eating disorders. In addition, if you live in a state of clutter (physically, mentally, or otherwise), this can greatly add to your stress levels negatively and trigger high levels of the stress hormone—cortisol.

An example of this is leaving your desk in a mess every day when you leave and then returning to that same mess the following morning. Or not making up your bed when you get up, do you just go sleep again in an unmade bed? You might even be feeling that you've got so much to do, and in your strive for perfectionism, you get nothing done because you feel like everything is a priority!

Individuals that are prone to cortisol imbalances will find themselves having high blood sugar and inflammation.

***Damien's tip****: For many people, the tidiness of their home and the current state of their mental well-being are directly correlated. If you've been feeling down for a few days, you can sometimes trick your brain into snapping out of it by getting your house sparkling clean. Following the previous patterns, the brain will assume that "the good days" have begun again.*

. . .

**10. Feeling Fake!** When you are in constant doubt of your own talents and capabilities, and you very seldom give praise to yourself, this is categorized as Imposter Syndrome! Feeling like you are fake can lead to all sorts of forms of self-sabotage.

An example of this is where you don't even attempt to work for and gain things you really want. Not going on a date with your crush and not getting a premium job offer because you feel unwanted and that "people won't want to hear what I have to say—I am not as successful as they are." The same goes for salary negotiations. When you do not believe in your own worth, you will most likely undersell yourself and, in that process, sabotage your financial strength.

Other symptoms of Impostor Syndrome include not setting boundaries (or not honoring them), being unable to stand up for yourself because you are under a misperception that people are merely tolerating you.

With self impostor syndrome raging, you will also struggle to take credit for the fantastic work you have done and sometimes feel like your true achievements are just luck. Keep reminding yourself that these things did not just land on a silver plate in front of you - you made it happen - own it!

**11. Being Overzealous and Overdoing Everything.**
The modern term here that coins this phrase is being

"extra." This implies that you are overcommitted and also contributes to different forms of self-sabotage. In other words, you set yourself up for failure! Let's face it, if you take on too much at once, you will either never be able to complete the task or will deliver sub-standard results. Alternatively, you will end up making personal sacrifices to make others happy.

An example of this would be deciding that you will be the sole planner of your best friend's baby shower. You agree you will order and pick up the cake, get the decorations, cook for the party, decorate the house, prepare the drinks, create and send invites for the guests, etc. All on top of your other full-time job commitments, a lift to the airport you agreed to give to your neighbor, looking after their dog when they are away, etc. If you are overcommitted continuously, you are not putting yourself first and therefore sabotaging your well-being. It will result in severe levels of stress and anxiety, low energy and fatigue—or worse. It is up to you to learn to say no, or there will always be someone asking you to "do just this one more thing." Or, every time the boss asks a favor, you always put your hand up first, even though this will take time out of that vacation you so desperately need! Take time for yourself - as many times as you have heard this - you are not a bad person for putting yourself first sometimes.

**12. Burnt out.** Examples of questions to ask yourself: Have you forgotten everyday things of late? Or have you been making more mistakes than usual? If you are constantly on edge and overtired, this can lead to what is defined as *burnout*.

.  .  .

Even if you plan everything to a tee, you will sometimes not do anything about it after the initial "burst of action." for example, let's say that you are perhaps embarking on a very big personal project. You may have been giving it all you got. However, when the novelty wears off, you feel that you simply *can't* continue, even though it can mean exciting things for you in the future; you simply lose interest after a while or have no more energy or will to continue.

This will also open you up to a plethora of mental and physical illnesses, as, in essence, you are driving a car without gas. Mentally you will have low moods and much lower than usual interest in anything (apathy), might feel irritable. You might also experience symptoms such as chronic migraines or debilitating headaches that seem not to want to go away in a physical sense.

**13. Financial Auto-Sabotage.** When it comes to money, many therapists are of the opinion that the majority of their patients appear to be embodying what they call financial self-sabotage. This is when the saboteur has an intense dislike or even distaste toward people they deem financially wealthy. They think rich people have no values. Therefore, when they start approaching the level where they could begin to perceive themselves as rich, they sabotage their finances as they do not want to belong in a demographic category they hate.

.  .  .

Their intense hatred seems to sprout from beliefs that the wealthy stand for everything wrong in the world, and it is often accompanied by using absolute words. Examples of absolute words are: "I am *never* going to be married," or "I am *always* the one to be overlooked for that promotion."

It is also because many people in life aspire to have some form of financial stability, and because they desire this so much, they envy the individuals that do manage to succeed financially. However, the saboteur does not realize that due to their constant procrastination and inability to work towards this goal, it will never become a reality for them. (MedCircle, 2021).

## 14. Negative dynamics in a previous relationship.

This might also have a part to play in your self-destructive behavior. For example, with an ex, you might've been belittled or abused when you spoke your mind. So instead of communicating to a new partner how you feel, you rather tend to keep quiet out of fear of history repeating itself.

You might think that not trying something is an impenetrable shield that will protect you from failure. Fear of failing will keep you from progressing in life and growth. The moment something goes wrong, you sit back feeling satisfied with yourself because again, "I was right, this was a bad idea." Sadly, the fact is that you are so motivated to self-sabotage, so you're not the least surprised when bad things come to pass.

. . .

**15. Avoiding conflict at all costs!** This ties in very closely to the form of self-sabotage we've discussed in the previous paragraph. Because you've "learned from the past," you tend to not engage in any form of conflict—much at the expense cost of putting yourself down, but "at least you are avoiding it"; therefore, you can't get hurt in the process. But, unfortunately, this will hamper you from reaching any goals in the future, no matter what they may be.

**16. Neglect or rejection in the past.** You might have been rejected or neglected or even abandoned by a care-giver or a partner in the past. This will not only cause low levels of self-esteem, but you will self-sabotage any relation-ship in the future in a bid to avoid feeling this exposed and vulnerable again in the future. That guy that said he loved you and that he would never leave, just for you to catch him in bed with your best friend... this makes you afraid of ever being in a committed relationship again, so you choose instead to have fun with the bad boys - because hey..." It's exciting and no commitment is required," or "I get to see him when he is available, so it means he wants me when he calls."

**17. Maladaptive behaviors linked to trauma.** In the past, you might've had to deploy a series of strategies that served a purpose and got you where you are now. However, you've become so accustomed to them helping you to survive that you are utterly oblivious to how they now aid your path of self-destruction. Maladaptive behavior is ubiquitous when trying to deal with traumas that have a heavy bearing on your life (Maladaptive behavior: Causes, connection to anxiety and treatment, n.d.).

These types of behaviors that have helped you adapt to situations in the past now become maladaptive because you continue using them as a crutch, even long after the storms have passed.

If you have experienced trauma earlier in life or as a young child, especially being used or abused by someone you've trusted, you might feel unsafe and unworthy of having good things in life. So you are inclined to self-destruct - often blaming yourself for circumstances entirely out of your control.

**18. Are you self-identifying as a control freak?** Do you have a constant need to be in control and sometimes even be a dictator? Certain types of self-sabotage will fuel this inner monster. For example, even when you are well aware that continuing to put something off will get you in trouble at work or otherwise, you would rather let it happen because regularly, in such a way, you feel like you are in control of the outcome.

Sometimes pushing your advice or opinions when it was not asked for will cause an intense dislike of people towards you! For example, your friend Pete does not have a weapon proficiency license as yet. However, they are well aware of the rules on the range, but you feel compelled to tell Pete what YOU think they should and shouldn't do because "I have my weapon proficiency license"- bottom line, don't be THAT person.

**19. Blaming others for your circumstances.** We've all experienced a situation (sometimes more than once) where an unfortunate series of circumstances simply just occur, without any human intention or even intervention.

However, if you are constantly seeking an outlet to rid yourself of the frustrations that you are experiencing by shifting the blame squarely on someone else's shoulders, then perhaps it's time that you take a step back and engage in some introspection to determine where you might've played a part in it.

Suppose you've just gone through a bad breakup. You were the one to break up with your then partner because you were at loggerheads about certain aspects of the relationship. Yet, after the initial shock, etc., has worn off, you actually feel good on the inside about letting this person go. Why? Because you feel that you've made the right decision because "they will never change."

You then get your *posse* together, badmouth the now ex, and your friends applaud you for your efforts in "getting out before it's too late." Although this might help ease the pain, you owe it to your future self to take some time to heal and dig very deep to see how you might've contributed negatively too. Otherwise, you are likely to struggle with the same issues again in the future! After all -

in most cases, you would have *chosen* to stay with that person for as long as you did. Many bits of ancient and not-so-ancient wisdom have captured the same idea in sayings like "double-bladed sword," "the coin has two sides," or "it takes two to tango." If possible, try to remain objective - it is never solely your fault, but it is never exclusively someone else's fault either.

**20. Hitting the eject button comes easy to you.** There is nothing wrong with making a 180-degree turn and walking away from something or someone that does not serve a purpose in your life. Sometimes, it is the only option that you have. But before you walk away, you should ask yourself if you've exhausted all other options.

For example, you might've changed jobs a few times over the last few years. You might've been unappreciated in job one. You might have been underpaid in the second job but were also expected to work long hours, etc. The above mentioned are all valid reasons; however, if you regularly engage in such a pattern throughout your life, you might find it hard to get the job you want because any prospective employers will doubt your commitment to your work.

If you tend to throw in the towel before grafting a bit and getting your elbows dirty, it might curb your ability to make better decisions in the future because you are too used to taking the easy way out.

. . .

**21. Dating people that aren't right for you.** When it comes to relationship sabotage, you might discover that you continuously date the type of people that are *wrong* for you. Examples of relationship auto-sabotage can include:

- Always sticking to dating types, for example, deciding only to date supermodel-types that constantly need your attention, hampering you from achieving your individual goals.
- Compromising all your ideals and dreams in an effort to make it work with someone.
- Remaining in a relationship, even though you are secretly unhappy and it is going nowhere slowly.

# 2

# In Harm's Way - The Iceberg of Self-Destruction

As we unpack this mountainous task of self-discovery and self-betterment, we have to take this massive iceberg and break it down into smaller chunks of ice. After doing so, we will melt these chunks of ice until there is nothing left but water to nourish our roots and get us growing as people again.

## The After-Tremors of Self-Sabotage

So what happens when we engage in activities whereby we self-sabotage?

In the first instance, we set ourselves up to fail by cultivating destructive behavioral patterns. These damaging habits derail any attempts to make our goals a reality.

Secondly, it is very harmful to your reputation and personal brand, your *street cred* if you will. Your boss, friends, partner, and everyone else around you will start seeing you as disrespectful, unreliable, a pushover, or untrustworthy.

Lastly, you may have difficulty in managing anger and lash out passive-aggressively every opportunity you get. Of course, this will destroy your relationships, but continuing in such a downtrend is what will eventually result in low self-esteem.

This continuous path of negative behavior will immediately summit you to the tip of the iceberg of self-destruction! Unfortunately, this means that we tend only to address the 20% that is visible but that we forget about the remainder of the 80% that is submerged deep in the water, which is where we should start digging and repairing ourselves first.

## Self-Destructive Behavior - A Diagnosis

Did you know that you might've developed auto-sabotaging strategies without even knowing? This is due to them serving you as a method of coping in life! A way to protect yourself and/or avoid pain.

Suppose you put yourself down when you don't get that promotion at work - This is deemed as self-destructive. This might be a result of previous neglect in your past. But by no means does it imply that you have a mental disorder. However, when you can see it for what it is, you can make advancements to replace self-sabotaging behaviorisms with something constructive instead.

When you are experiencing such an overwhelming feeling of self-destruction that self-harming becomes a habit of gratification—you are dealing with an entirely different demon altogether! There are severe repercussions attached to this behavior, and if you find yourself in this type of situation, it is definitely time to seek some form of professional help.

Your first step would be to schedule a visit with a qualified therapist. This professional will engage in an interview-type setting with you to gain insight and understand the origins of your behavior and in a bid to determine if you might have a mental disorder of sorts. They will try to establish what you would like to achieve with the session and see if they can help you with it.

Some signs of non-suicidal self-harm include:

1. You were physically hurting yourself for five days or more in the past year.
2. You are harming yourself to feel good about yourself or as a means to forget negative feelings.
3. Being preoccupied with self-harm or constantly feeling the need to hurt yourself physically or emotionally - especially if you think you deserve pain.

4. You are feeling distressed about hurting yourself.

Self-harm and other forms of self-sabotage and self-destruction start as non-regular occurrences, but if left untreated, they can quickly escalate to habits—and bad ones at that!

## What Are The Dangers of Self-Destructive Behavior?

Studies have proven that harming oneself is prevalent in individuals who have a mental health diagnosis and those who don't. Of course, it can happen to any person of any age group, but these same studies have shown that it is common in teenagers and young adults.

Self-destruction can also originate from mental health disorders such as:

**Anxiety -** This is when you experience constant fear, stress, and worry. A *lot* of worry.

**Depression -** It is categorized by overwhelming feelings of being sad and disinterested all of the time.

**Eating disorders -** Some forms of eating disorders include bulimia, binge eating, and anorexia.

. . .

**Personality disorders -** There are a variety of different ways in which personality disorders can manifest themselves. Still, in general, it is feelings of not fitting in or having trouble relating to other people.

**Post-traumatic stress disorders (PTSD) -** This is a form of anxiety brought on by a traumatic experience in your past. It is a common occurrence in war veterans and victims of abuse.

When you come to terms with the fact that auto-sabotage did once serve some sort of purpose in your life, it forms your departure point in changing those destructive habits into something valuable and purposeful that yields actual meaning! More about this in the next chapter.

Did you know that there are two main types of self-sabotage?

## The Two Types of Self-Sabotage

Before we can delve into this section further, I need to highlight the two different types of self-sabotage that exist, namely:

- Conscious self-sabotage
- Unconscious self-sabotage

**Conscious self-sabotage.** Conscious self-sabotage is when you are fully aware of how negative your habits are and that they are aiding and abetting the fire by fueling the process of undermining your values and your dreams.

Example: *"I know that I have to prepare for tomorrow's meeting, but I don't feel like doing the research and compiling the stats."*

**Unconscious self-sabotage.** Unconscious self-sabotage is when you are not aware that your actions and bad habits are causing you harm.

Example: *You are a student skipping lectures and leaving coursework for the last minute. This way, you have an excuse of "I didn't really try hard" when you fail your exams because failing after studying properly would be too hard of a hit to take. You are not making a conscious decision to do this as there is no "grand plan" to build an excuse in your conscious thoughts.*

## Symptoms of Self-Sabotage And How to Treat Them

Some forms of self-destructive behavior are more obvious than others, and examples include:

1. Attempting to commit suicide.
2. Binge eating or going on periods of fasting if you feel repulsed by food.
3. Any compulsive behavior such as gaming for hours on end, engaging in gambling, or grudge shopping.
4. Risque sexual behavior.

5. Abusing drugs and alcohol.
6. Self-harming by cutting, burning yourself, or even literally pulling out your bodily hair.

There are less apparent vessels of self-sabotage too, which you might not realize that you are doing at first–speaking from a conscious level and some instances include:

- Constantly putting yourself down by saying you are not good enough.
- Being a people-pleaser or a brown noser just to fit in.
- Being a clingy person towards people who have no interest in you.
- Displaying behavior that is aggressive and which tends to alienate those around you.
- Maladaptive tendencies such as being passive-aggressive or avoiding everything at a chronic level.
- Constantly feeling sorry for yourself and reveling in pity parties.

The levels of severity and the frequency of these saboteur tendencies will be different for each individual. Some may experience infrequent mild feelings, and for others, they may occur more often and at a more intense level. But, no matter the form, shape, severity, or frequency, it is always dangerous and causes a multitude of problems.

## Suggested Treatment Options for Self-Sabotage

We will delve deep into various solutions in further chapters, as we want to give you as many options as possible to ensure you can utilize the things that you will personally find most acceptable and effective. First, however, we would like to touch on a vast array of options available so that you know that self-sabotage is not something you cannot alter/change. An effective treatment plan that targets your specific issues lies at the epicenter of discovery and recovery. And this means getting to the root cause of the issue. For example:

- Why do I feel the need or compulsion to gamble?
- Why am I spending money buying stuff I don't need?
- Why am I hiding away from family and friends?

Forms of treatment include:

**Holistic therapies.** This includes any forms of supplementary self-care that will enhance additional treatment outcomes. These are classified as anything that relaxes and soothes you and brings about a peaceful state of being. Today, it even goes as far as including mental health treatment. Examples include:

1. Acupuncture

2. Aromatherapy
3. Art
4. Equine therapy
5. Guided meditation classes
6. Massage therapy
7. Meditation
8. Music therapy
9. Practicing mindfulness
10. Yoga

**Lifestyle counseling.** Here, saboteurs get educated on how to improve their overall wellness and how to make healthy lifestyle choices. This includes drafting a fitness plan, getting a better night's sleep, and changing their diet. It might come as a surprise to you to learn that all of these factors impact your mental wellness, and learning how to create healthy habits is a crucial component of effective treatment strategies.

For many auto-saboteurs, their behaviors are a call for assistance. Unfortunately, they might not be aware that they are harming themselves and others and how bad the future will be if they don't consciously choose to change them. Every person deserves to receive help and guidance when they need it the most!

**Psychotherapy.** This forms the primary basis of treating those saboteurs who engage in practices of self-harm. Therapy should be viewed as your safe space to work through emotional trauma–whether it is a result of loss and grief, an issue from your past such as abuse, an event that has caused you tremendous pain, or any deep-seated relationship drawbacks.

**Psychosocial education.** In this instance, you may gain a lot by improving on relatable skills. This includes emotional self-regulation and conflict resolution tools. In addition, understanding the problem better often helps many find easier ways to gain control over the said problem.

It all starts with changing your habits holistically!

## What Are Habits?

Habits are little daily rituals based on decisions that you make and the actions that you perform. Researchers at Duke University have found that habits make up 40 percent of our behavioral patterns on a daily basis (Clear, 2018).

The negative space where you find yourself today is a culmination of how bent out of shape your life has become. That which you perform on repeat every day forms the type of person you are, the things you stand for and believe in, and your current personality type.

Going from procrastination to productivity and negativity to positivity starts by improving your habits by distin-guishing between bad and good habits. If you can learn and grasp how to better your daily routines, you can truly transform your entire life.

## Healthy Habits vs. Unhealthy Habits

***Bad Habits.*** Unhealthy habits are the daily rituals that disrupt your life and stop you from achieving your goals. They bring about menace and risk, sap your time and energy, and have serious consequences such as ill-health and drainage of your physical being.

No matter the causes, bad habits should be replaced and not eliminated. They come in many types and forms.

## 13 Common Bad Habits Worth to Dispel out of Your Life

1. Stress eating. This can include overeating or even fasting in some cases.
2. Biting your nails.
3. Hanging out with people that have a negative outlook on life.
4. Being around those that don't appreciate the person that you are.
5. Smoking.
6. Drinking excessively.
7. Eating junk food.
8. Watching too much TV.
9. Spending copious amounts of time on social media.
10. Constantly being late.
11. Remaining in toxic relationships.

12. Leaving things until the very last minute.
13. Always focussing on the negative aspects of life.

You can agree that none of those mentioned above serve you any helpful purpose. So what are some of the good habits that we can replace these bad habits with?

***Good Habits.*** Healthy habits are positive forms of behavior that you conduct daily. They are meaningful and add balance to your life. So, what habits are categorized as positive habits?

## 25 Healthy Habits Worth Practicing as Often as Possible!

1. Engaging in activities such as meditation to form a deeper connection with yourself.
2. Enjoying some quality time outdoors.
3. Reading books on genres that you love or ones that serve as a means of self-help.
4. Getting enough sleep every night.
5. Appreciating your gifts and expressing gratitude towards the things you do have.
6. Finding one or even a few new hobbies and making time to engage in them often.
7. Smiling - you'd be amazed at how good it makes you feel(if not right away, then eventually)!
8. Performing activities that positively stimulate your brain.

9. Speaking kindly to others and yourself.
10. Exercising regularly.
11. Talk and reiterate positive affirmations.
12. Consuming a well-balanced diet.
13. Spending time with friends and family.
14. Living a life that has purpose and one that serves you!
15. Volunteering your time to a worthy cause.
16. Spending time with someone lonely, such as the senior folk.
17. Having a meal with family or loved ones.
18. Engaging in daily good hygiene practices.
19. Watching a feel-good movie or a comedy (in a healthy frequency, of course - no binging!).
20. Building a passive income.
21. Taking your to-do list and simplifying it.
22. Journaling.
23. Taking stock of the past week and reflecting on how you can improve the following week.
24. Enjoy a date night - even if it is just once a month.
25. Pay it forward by doing something kind every day. This can be for a cause, someone else, and don't forget yourself in the process!

As you can see, with little to no effort, some of the bad habits can be replaced with healthy ones. It might not be easy to do at first, but if you start small, you will be on such a high that you will seek more ways of incorporating this into your daily life.

## The Prognosis of Self-Sabotage And Self-Destructive Behavior

The good news is that it's not all doom and gloom. Even though auto-destructive behaviors can lead to severe mental breakdowns and health issues, you can completely heal and recover from your self-destructive tendencies if you decide to make a change for the better.

So how long will this healing process take exactly? Well, it will depend on an array of factors such as:

1. The severity and frequency of your particular symptoms.
2. Whether you are prone to other conditions associated with similar behavior such as PTSD and/or depression.
3. Your inclinations being linked to components such as eating disorders and alcohol/substance abuse.

## Areas in Our Lives Negatively Impacted by Self-Sabotage

**Intimate/romantic auto-sabotage.** Saboteurs will frequently do things that will wear away any long-term intimate relationship prospects, which in the end will only lead to heartache and loneliness. This is often born out of fear of loss.

Self-sabotaging in the romantic sense often involves:

- Blaming a partner
- Looking for fights
- Giving a partner the silent treatment
- Constantly checking a partner's behavior
- Controlling them
- Being clingy
- Having standards that are too high that the partner can't possibly live up to, and
- Just leaving relationships prematurely before they had a chance to develop.

Craving a fulfilled romantic partnership is part of our software. Here, people who auto-sabotage continuously upload or install toxic romantic relationships to their hardware even when such relationships are not conducive to either party, and there is no mutual respect. Instead, they'd rather harm themselves by remaining in these relationships because they can say they are *not* single or can see no way out.

Many saboteurs struggle to be alone and at peace with themselves, and they'd rather be in a destructive relationship as opposed to being single. This is because for a saboteur to be single, it will imply that they are alone! And in turn, it means that they are not happy. Alternatively, it is often a self-esteem issue, where victims of abusive relationships do not feel like they deserve any better. So if they make some really bad choices when picking a partner, the other half may actually be intentionally aiming to destroy their self-esteem due to various issues of their own (e.g., narcissism, abandonment issues, etc.)

Clinical Psychologist Nick Wignall and Sexual and Reproductive Health Researcher Anabelle Bernard Fournier wrote that saboteurs who romantically sabotage themselves all have identical patterns attached to their behavior. However, these patterns can manifest in very different symptoms.

**Career self-sabotage.** This is where saboteurs will engage in any activity that prevents them from achieving career goals. Anxiety and fear of failure can put them in comfort zones that prevent them from advancing up the ladder, despite harboring a desire to do precisely that. In turn, this leads to being unhappy at work, an unhealthy mental state, and in most cases, these self-sabotagers will often change jobs.

**Educational self-sabotage.** This form of self-sabotage can either be intentional or unintentional (conscious or unconscious). It comprises a series of patterns and behaviors that explain why a student performs poorly or fails. The root cause is often a lack of self-confidence and/or anxiety spells. Failure can then be blamed on factors such as procrastination or just not trying at all. In most cases, it's not an inherent lack of ability but rather a reflection of choice.

· · ·

**Auto-sabotaging social relationships.** In this area of a saboteur's life, they are often motivated by an inclination to feel like they are in constant competition by needing to prove their equality, superiority, or worth. Often these actions will result in them exercising control over other people to win their approval. Negative behaviors linked to sabotaging social relationships with family and friends can manifest as:

- Passive-aggressive tendencies
- Constantly seeking approval
- Giving false compliments
- Being clingy
- Bragging
- Complaining a lot
- Always asking someone if they are upset or angry with them.

## Amukelani's Story - Self-Diagnosis of the Procrastinator

*This is a true story of a very real person - the name and personal details have been changed to maintain anonymity. Amukelani is a self-identified saboteur in the main form of a Procrastinator.*

He has created a self-awareness that the problem exists in his daily life as it has embedded itself into his existence as a pattern of continuous behavior. Amu has agreed to share his story to help others achieve the same awareness, and as a result, help others make the first steps forward.

. . .

**Amu's Troubles.** There were a few key things in his behavior that Amu has identified as symptoms of self-sabotage: **excessive procrastination, missed opportunities, and lowered self-esteem**. Subsequently, such symptoms have resulted in multiple missed opportunities, and he feels he lost out–BIG TIME! Through the years, he has had several light bulb moments that made him realize that this is something that he needs to work on, or it will destroy his life if he lets the self-sabotaging tendencies get the better of him.

**The Pressure to Perform and The Procrastination.** After retrospectively unpacking the causes behind his self-sabotage, Amu sat back and admitted to himself that he was the main reason for not achieving the things he wanted from life. His biggest issue? Procrastinating and leaving important tasks to the absolute last minute - especially when it came to pursuing a career in Mechanical Engineering.

His undergrad course was intense and required pouring over many hours of course content at home, which needed to be presented to his lecturers and peers. Yet, even knowing this, he continued the downward spiral by saying to himself- "I'll *get it done later.*"

I know what you're thinking - so many people we all know do the exact same thing! You could say Amu was consciously sabotaging himself as he was well aware of the coursework demands but still went ahead and set himself up for failure by achieving average results at best!

. . .

Knowing the detrimental outcome, he would chastise himself to say, "*Next time, I would start work early.*" Like how you hear people saying, "*from next Monday I will eat healthier*" - next Monday comes, and many decide that "*next Monday*" will be fine and the cycle keeps going. Or, as you will often hear procrastinators say in Spain, "**mañana**" - literally it means "*tomorrow,*" but in a matter of expression, it means later, which could be referring to next week or some years later - no defined time when exactly.

When Amu delved deeper into his sense of self-awareness, he admitted that after self-reflecting, this was partially due to the coursework demands and partially due to pressure from his parents to perform. Such pressure often results in people becoming extra harsh on themselves, feeling defeated and thinking, "*there's no point in trying at all.*"

When Amukelani turned seven years of age, he was enrolled in a program for gifted children, and as a result, the family's expectations of him skyrocketed. Kids being kids, he didn't understand the impact and pressure of such high expectations at the time.

This pressure for excellent performance from his parents still has a lasting negative impact on his life today! In Amu's case, being part of an African family played a big part, too - raising kids and utilizing a very direct and strict approach is an entirely standard thing to observe in their culture. But, looking back, he felt that it might've been different if they had employed another way and style of communicating their thoughts and concerns to him.

Kids being kids, he didn't stick to the program for long as he saw no value in it. As a direct result, being the recipient of threats such as *"If you don't do this, you won't succeed later in life"* became Amu's belief. Because he had heard it repeated often enough, his mindset was nurtured to think that unless X, Y, and Z happened - he would fail.

In his parent's defense, it is likely that Amu's parents were acting based on what is known in behavioral sociology as modeling. Modeling is a way of adopting behaviors - it most commonly refers to mimicking the behaviors of those around you, and it is one of the most common ways children learn. So it's not that they did this on purpose or didn't love him enough; they simply didn't know any better - they most likely grew up with the same treatment! Unknowingly, his parents didn't take care of his well-being.

After leaving the "buffer" of home, he looked at the other students and kept asking himself the question, *"Why is everyone else so well adjusted, apart from me?"*. Amu used to think that if you grew up strict, you would have your shit together and have strong self-discipline by then and, as a result, be able to *adult* better and adjust to the demands of being a grown-up faster.

Today, Amukelani feels that this is almost entirely the opposite. Overbearing parents and keeping others happy caused a disconnect in himself from enjoying being a student and wanting to succeed later in life.

**Amukelani Today.** Amu has discovered and implemented mechanisms to deal with his self-sabotaging tendencies. The method of outweighing what needs to be done and the future rewards it holds became his life raft. Amu approaches this so-called *reward-seeking system* by focussing on his two primary goals, which are:

- To move up the ladder in his workplace or find a better-paying, more enjoyable job.
- Being healthier and getting fit.

This time around (call it a second chance), he aims to do things for himself and regularly takes stock of his progress. He started a new job recently and aims to progress up the corporate ladder in the next year. His backup plan if he can't do that? Find another workplace once he has upskilled and gained more experience. Best of all? Amu's new job makes him feel that there are other ways to succeed without being a doctor or an engineer!

Amu had to train himself to get out of his comfort zone as it didn't come naturally. He was not a risk-taker earlier in this life, and the thought of trying something new caused him great angst in the past. However, the moment Amu was able to see the benefit of **the calling**– he managed to burst his self-comfort bubble and got much closer to finding his purpose.

**How did Amu get the confidence to leave his comfort bubble?** He put in the effort and the hard work (even to this day) to *recondition* his mind to say that it's ok to leave those "safe" confines. The moment he feels that familiar fear of the unknown coming along, he preps his mind to face it head-on instead of turning the other way! (He consciously resists the resistance).

What exactly brought these changes on? Well, Amu decided that he had enough of working long hours, being mistreated at this old job, and realizing it served him no purpose! But he knew nothing would change unless he took action! So we can say that Amu's push for a better life came from negative triggers.

One of the things that he has also realized is that when he feels lazy, he tends to procrastinate against getting things done. So, as a solution, he started going to bed earlier - he has cultivated a good habit of getting enough quality sleep throughout the night. In turn, the additional energy boost has enabled him to perform at peak during the day and make the most of it. In addition to that, he started going out and meeting new people to broaden his network instead of playing video games.

Furthermore, Amu latched onto fitness as a coping mechanism at first. This way, he felt he was seen and respected by people by allowing him to stand his ground and not feel awkward in public. He started powerlifting, where he discovered a natural affinity for lifting weights. In fact, he got so good at it that he began winning competitions. Unfortunately, he had to stop due to an injury, but now, it's an essential part of his daily routine, helping him to become more confident, fit, and healthy.

By putting himself out there, he discovered a natural ability and made it work for him. The physical change he saw in his body brought about the confidence boost he so desperately wanted! Others noticed this change, and he also started feeling more comfortable in his own skin.

**What Amu's advice is to his younger self?** Get outside, meet people, and do things–a lot more! Stop spending time with things that have no meaning that won't matter when you are older, and experience the benefits that life has to offer! Get to interact more with people, learn new things, do things you've never done and see your character development blossom into the beautiful, unique, worthy person you are intended to be!

**His advice to other gifted children?** Take care not to self-sabotage by suffering from burnout. In his opinion, it's vital for a talented person not to succumb to the pressures of expectation from those around you. Instead, spend some time each day studying in your earlier years to allow you to cope with the pressures and demands young adult and adult life will throw your way!

# 3

# Why We Do It

*"We all have 'issues', because we all have a story. And no matter how much work you've done on yourself, we all snap back sometimes. So be easy on you. Growth is a dance. Not a light switch."* - (Kim, n.d.).

## Hardware And Software of The Mind

Did you know that at the moment, the human brain is the most powerful computer in existence today? Even the scientists agree on that! However, sometimes something so powerful can be both a blessing and a burden in disguise.

In most cases, we can't calculate faster than the average computer, and in other cases, we are inferior to the advances of Artificial Intelligence (AI). That being said, our brain works all sorts of wonders that man-made computers are still not capable of. In essence, your brain and your body are the hardware. You will know that you can have the most up-to-date computer, but the hardware is rendered useless if not coupled with compatible software.

We don't get to pick the hardware; our bodies come with their own properties - good and not so good. Even some of the basic "software" is already pre-installed - like a brand new computer that you buy with a pre-installed operating system. Therefore, processes often run in our minds that we do not fully understand or perceive as something out of our control.

This brings us to the software component. It is, of course, our mind, and like a computer, our mind needs to constantly update the software to keep it going and functioning at optimal levels. This also means an alteration in terms of installing those habits and things that serve us well and uninstalling the bad.

Forms of alteration include:

- Changing our habits (sometimes for the good and other times for the bad).
- Learning new skills and growing as a person.
- Forgetting information over the course of time.
- Fixing fragmented/damaged chunks of our mind.
- And, sometimes, we bury information somewhere deep inside because it causes us pain, and we'd rather not have to deal with it.

Like with software, it is only natural that we constantly push our minds to the limit in installing and uninstalling updates. In turn, it will create glitches, or as a software developer will call it - a bug! Examples of these include things like traumatic experiences and/or fears.

As a result, these so-called bugs then prevent our hardware AND software from functioning at full capacity and often cause breaks in our human programming. For example, self-sabotage, binge eating, and procrastination start to manifest themselves, and you begin to feel so overwhelmed that although you've got much to do, you end up not doing anything at all!

The good news is that you already possess the required hardware to manage your life and the ones that will make for a smooth existence! The only thing you need to do is consciously decide to deploy these hardware mechanisms and nurture them. We will do so by taking a deep dive into the main reasons why our hardware malfunctions and which triggers (bugs) make us auto-sabotage and eventually embark on a tumultuous path of self-destruction. Self-sabotage is essentially a firewall that our body created by these bugs (glitches created by our upbringing, traumatic experiences, learned negative behaviors, etc.). Therefore in order to avoid any additional bugs, our system installs patches that sometimes keep us in the comfort zone. We can then say that auto-sabotage is kin to a bug-induced self-preservation trigger whereby we react automatically.

Perhaps a complex analogy, but read along, and it will start making more sense.

## 8 Reasons Behind Our Self-Sabotage

Some saboteurs feel they are getting in their own way. Some call it self-defeating behaviors, and others deem it as shooting yourself in the foot. Whatever your understanding of self-sabotage is, you can ensure you don't reach your goals when you sabotage yourself.

As we've already discussed, there are countless ways in which we sabotage ourselves. In some cases, these behavioral patterns are sneaky because, at first, they are minor issues—one game of League of Legends before studying. In the moment, this action might even come across as helpful— "to help relieve stress," we justify!

So why do we tend to do this to ourselves? Each person is unique and may have their own wombo-combo of what effed them up, but here are eight big common reasons.

### 1. Self-Esteem - The Relationship Between Self-Sabotage and Low *Amour Propre*

*Amour-Propre* means self-love in French. It is important to highlight the toxic link that self-sabotage has to low self-esteem. Constantly viewing yourself in a negative light and putting yourself down will turn your life into a runaway train of negative prophecies that are self-fulling! When we fail to believe in ourselves, our abilities, and our gifts, we create a carefully woven web where the deadly spider of self-sabotage is waiting to trap us like a fly.

If sticking to the relationship theme, it might be that you are not good enough for a great partner, you do everything wrong, you will not find better, etc. In turn, this pushes our romantic interests or partners away, or we accept being mistreated - telling ourselves that this is our only option.

Overall, it is a direct result of the false perception that somehow we deserve this bad treatment—again, installing software into our minds that will lead to a bug called low self-esteem. When this happens, whatever code (action) you are trying to run that requires self-esteem (which is literally most of our actions) - you will get a buggy outcome because a component (self-esteem specifically) within that code is broken or missing. In another analogy, it's like cooking a meal and forgetting to add any salt or spices - you are bound to end up with something bland that will taste sub-standard.

As you can see, this is a vicious cycle of self-destruction whereby the person is presented with a challenge like everyone else but avoids tackling it headfirst because they lack the self-esteem to stand up against adversity. In turn, this leads to nothing other than a generally pessimistic outlook on life where they feel they aren't deserving of good things, and this causes them to stay dormant.

· · ·

Instead, they would rather remain in the confines of their comfort bubble because they deem it as being safe. They will never even try to push their limits because they feel that it will never work out for them anyway! Sometimes, when they are fed up enough, they will put in a half-assed effort. However, because of the fear of success, they will likely never push through with enough momentum - withdrawing the impactful swing needed. Like thinking that their fist would get hurt, rather than envisioning themselves mentally punching right through the wall, they've built up themselves.

One of the most painful things to watch in the behaviors of self saboteurs is the opportunities flying right past them. People with low self-esteem tend to create reasons that validate procrastination, and therefore such opportunities pass by untouched. Of course, in a relationship sense, disagreements will arise. Still, individuals with a lack of *amour propre* (self-esteem) won't take any initiative to resolve the disagreement and would rather let it fester, causing distance in their romantic relationship.

It has been proven that individuals with low self-esteem are unaware that this is the exact root cause of other problems in their lives. Therefore, we need to do our utmost to sabotage the link between self-sabotage and low self-esteem!

## 2. No Self-Worth

. . .

What makes self-worth different from self-esteem is that you don't recognize that you are an individual deserving and worthy of good things when lacking self-worth. As we've unpacked above, self-esteem is what you believe, think, and how you feel about yourself. They are closely related yet different.

Saboteurs tend to categorize themselves into houses of where they fit in society—think similarly to getting assigned a house in Harry Potter. These categories are self-limiting, meaning they put themselves where they think they belong. These proverbial societal boxes are defined by factors such as family status, your parents' occupations, and what society thinks of you, to name a few examples. Saboteurs then pick one or more of these boxes where they feel worthy of fitting into. They tend to avoid the boxes they think they don't fit into and self-sabotage themselves, thinking they are punching above their weight.

Strange enough, many people tend to work their fingers to the bone and aim high in an attempt to make up for feeling inadequate. Sadly, when their efforts do pay off, they self-sabotage and self-destruct. But why?

Well, in many cases, the answer lies in a concept known as cognitive dissonance. People like to be consistent. Normally their actions are directly correlated with their values and belief systems. When this trifecta does not align, people get unsettled and then throw the applecart out in an attempt to force them to align.

. . .

This is how we sabotage ourselves because when the good things start happening for us, but we don't love and appreciate ourselves as individuals, we then hit the eject button prematurely to eliminate the dissonance. It then feels horrible to fail, but not as bad as it does when we do succeed if we fear success.

## 3. Lack of Self-Acceptance

Having self-acceptance, embracing who you are, and believing in yourself plays a vital role in all areas of your life including, romantic and social relationships, school/studies, and work. When you can look at yourself by means of a positive lens will aid you to create and pursue the life you so deeply desire and deserve. In addition to that, your overall health and well-being will dramatically improve if you have a healthy outlook on life.

When you have a dislike for the person you are currently, or you believe that other people don't like the real *you*-not only are you trying to put on a constant show for them—exhausting your energy resources, but you are also putting yourself under a tremendous amount of pressure and stress by constantly injecting that cortisol straight into your bloodstream.

This could be something as minor as being a guy that loves rom-com movies but never admitting this to a group of male friends in fear of them perceiving you as less masculine. It can also be something more significant, like not accepting that you were born gay and attracted to the same sex.

Each individual is full of their own little weird intricacies. Someone once said to me: *"If someone appears 100% 'normal' with absolutely nothing unusual about them, they are either extremely boring or hiding something"*-Just some food for thought! These "weirdnesses," so to speak, should be accepted and embraced.

Your self-beliefs, abilities, feelings, and thoughts are all factors that affect your daily decisions and impact how you view those around you and the universe in general. For example, your self-acceptance could well be the factor determining decisions such as choosing a specific career path, which studies you want to pursue or working towards that hard-earned promotion, trying a new hobby, or asking your crush out on a date. Let's face it; nobody wants a bad opinion of themselves standing in the way of reaching goals and living a life of fulfillment!

Working towards reconnecting with yourself, building your self-acceptance, and loving yourself again is not something fixed. Instead, it should be viewed as something on a continuum, which means you can improve your life for the better.

Therapies such as counseling can aid in improving the acceptance of self. If you struggle with embracing yourself for who you are, the chances are good that you've cultivated a negative inner dialog or that you engage in negative self-talk frequently. Counseling can transform destructive self-talk, which is hurtful but teaches you to speak to your inner being more compassionately.

Having compassion means that you need to be forgiving and kind to yourself and avoid constantly tapping yourself over the knuckles by being too critical. Self-compassion goes a long way and can lead you to have a healthy relationship of love, gratitude, and acceptance of yourself as a person.

Renowned author, Ph.D. Professor and Licensed Master Social Worker(LMSW) Brené Brown, at the University of Houston has dedicated her life to understanding why we struggle to believe that we are enough and how that paints a cultural portrait of self-worth. She has also delved deep into her books about what fuels this innate feeling that we have to be perfect all of the time and that vulnerability has no place in our lives. However, at the end of the day, she believes that no matter how much was done or how it was done–YOU ARE ENOUGH! You are worthy of joy, belonging, and love. She is a firm believer that the idea of wholeheartedness stems from interacting with the world from a place called worthiness of self (Sounds True, 2012).

## 4. Obsession With Control

In this instance, we are referring to the proverbial control freak in colloquial terms. This is a person that would rather be in the driving seat when it comes to failure, as opposed to allowing it to catch them off-guard.

When the feeling of what they perceive as an imminent threat becomes overwhelming, they take control of the situation. This form of self-sabotage isn't nice, but saboteurs view it as a noble substitute instead of spinning out of control. They feel that if they're at the wheel, they'd rather watch it all be consumed by flames, but the actual burn feels well-controlled to them.

The control freak or so-called A-Type personality is acting out of fear of losing control. This can also present in more severe forms where it forms part of a personality disorder where saboteurs undermine others by deploying controlling behavior. This then permits them to act out by dictating the order of situations and outcomes. Individuals who struggle with the need to be in control have an innate fear of being at the mercy of other individuals.

How do you know when you are a control freak? Ask yourself these questions:

- Do you feel that you have to be in control of all circumstances and outcomes in your life?
- Do you find yourself constantly stressed out when you aren't always in control?
- Do you have difficulty trusting other people with tasks because you are worried they might not do it right?

- Do you feel the need to be in control of every situation and/or relationship because your trust has been broken in the past?
- Have you been modeled as a child or young adult by your parents to the point where you always have to take the initiative and conduct the orchestra out of fear of disappointment and punishment?

Control freaks, so to speak, have certain habits and characteristics about them that make other people not want to be around them. Some of these habits include:

***Not understanding why people can't see things the way that you do.*** Many saboteurs have a problem called being perspective-limited. What do I mean by this? These individuals fail to see things any differently than what they already do. They view life through a single lens that they have created for themselves. They are not capable of even remotely considering the fact that if they were to be thoughtful people, they would have the ability to see things differently. Saboteurs also feel if people disagree with them, they are wrong.

***Control freaks get cross if people don't follow their advice.*** We have all been in situations before, where we give someone genuine advice. Some people will use your advice, and others won't - and there's no issue with that. A controlling person would straight-up ask you if you acted on their advice, and if you didn't, they will get mad and will probably lash out at you for not following their advice and wasting their time asking for it. Ironically, it is likely they have given the advice without being asked.

***Controlling people expect others to follow their rules.*** So these self-sabotagers have a set of universal rules they've created for themselves and which they will impose on other people. It doesn't matter what others think of these rules, but control freaks will judge them based on adherence anyway.

***Controlling people never think they are controlling.*** You can't argue with a control freak, and no matter how hard you try to diffuse the situation, they are not approachable about the fact that you want to highlight their ways in the most subtle of ways; they simply just won't hear of it. In addition, control freaks have an issue with accepting the worldview of others and won't be open to seeing the light that the people around them might have different perspectives and their own points of view.

## 5. Feeling Like a Fraud - Impostor Syndrome

Saboteurs up the ante by engaging in activities such as taking on bigger tasks with more responsibility that puts them in the public spotlight; they tend to feel that they have that much more to lose, the higher they try to rise. They start doing what needs to be done, but when all eyes turn on them, they immediately question their choices and want out.

. . .

They think that if they bring attention to themselves and their skills and don't become successful at it, they will be branded as a fraud. Almost 100% of the time, these thoughts are only in their own heads. This term is coined as Impostor Syndrome. How does Impostor Syndrome rear its ugly head? By doing as little as possible and flying under the radar, or pushing yourself hard and having that nagging worry in the back of the head that you are going to be called out.

Impostor Syndrome has the dangerous tendency to lead straight to procrastination and either consciously or unconsciously seeking what you perceive as the solitude of engaging in activities that distract you from your goals.

These feelings of doubting yourself are persistent and persuasive. It's also called fraud syndrome, impostor experience, or perceived fraudulence.

**6. That Crave for Familiarity.** Rather the devil that you know than the one that you don't, right? Wrong! Because saboteurs tend to stay in their comfort zone, they tend to pick consistency over their own happiness, time and again!

For me, C.Joybell.C explained the best of what it feels like to live outside the comfort zone. It's so powerful that it still resonates with me today!

.  .  .

*"I have realized; it is during the times I am far outside my element that I experience myself the most. That I see and feel who I really am, the most! I think that's what a comet is like, you see, a comet is born in the outer realms of the universe! But it's only when it ventures too close to our sun or to other stars that it releases the blazing "tail" behind it and shoots brazen through the heavens! And meteors become sucked into our atmosphere before they burst like firecrackers and realize that they're shooting stars! That's why I enjoy taking myself out of my own element, my own comfort zone, and hurling myself out into the unknown. Because it's during those scary moments, those unsure steps taken, that I am able to see that I'm like a comet hitting a new atmosphere: suddenly I illuminate magnificently, and fire dusts begin to fall off of me! I discover a smile I didn't know I had, I uncover a feeling that I didn't know existed in me... I see myself. I'm a shooting star—a meteor shower. But I'm not going to die out. I guess I'm more like a comet then. I'm just going to keep on coming back."*
(Comfort Zone Quotes [290 quotes], 2011).

For example, suppose you are sadly used to being abused, ignored, or neglected. In that case, you tend to get a sadistic sense of comfort and keep putting yourself back into that scenario— because it's familiar to you—sacrificing your happiness in the process.

But you have to tell yourself that when self-sabotage tendencies come around, you have to target the root of the problem to weed it out—in this case—you have a fear of failure!

.  .  .

**7. Seeking Something or Someone to Blame for Your Misfortune.** When things don't work out for saboteurs, they forget to do introspection and will put the blame squarely on the shoulders of the self-sabotage vessel instead of themselves. Thoughts like *"He broke up with me—because we fought all of the time"*.

Sure, these reasons might be valid, but they are superficial, and blaming others is a deflecting mechanism. We do this because we don't want to own up to our *shit* (more on how in a later chapter), as well as in an attempt to deflect the attention away from ourselves.

Sure it might've started innocently, when you did something wrong, but when Dad asked *"who did it,"* you probably pointed a dirty little finger at one of your siblings. You did this because you didn't want to deal with any adverse consequences where you knew you were in trouble. As innocent as it was then, the pattern of deflective behavior can morph into a psychological auto-defense mechanism.

Deflection could also have manifested after the childhood development phase. This is where you did not blame others but felt nervous about a scenario, and you didn't want someone to be cross with you. So deflection can happen consciously or unconsciously. Whatever the root cause of the problem, it's crucial that you stop engaging in behavioral deflection patterns and start taking ownership of your mistakes or avoiding difficult situations.

. . .

Closely related to deflection is the projection phase. Projection is also passing the buck onto others, with the exception of making them feel unwanted feelings. Examples include piling your anxiety onto them, guilt-tripping them into getting something you want, and other negative emotions. Another example is where one partner in an intimate relationship is cheating but is seeking ways of accusing the non-cheating partner of infidelity (healthline, n.d.). But why do we deflect or project? Because no one wants to look like an asshole or feel like one. We don't want the people around us to have a negative perception of us. Instead, we want them to look up to us in high regard. This very much ties in with craving acceptance from others.

We constantly feel we need to make ourselves look better because we don't want to feel inadequate and be known for making errors. Living a life where you try not to make mistakes is *highly* impossible. We are human, and therefore sometimes, we will have to face punishment or negative consequences as a result of our actions. Making mistakes is 100% normal, and we should not create ego defenses in a bid not to look bad to others because this will harm them emotionally.

Deflection is also a coping mechanism deployed by saboteurs to ensure that people don't think less of them. The intent might not be to cause harm, and they might not want to look perfect, but they sure as hell don't want to look stupid! Saboteurs deflect because they want to stay in people's good books and are afraid of what will happen if people knew they made a mistake and might even feel bad if their deflection gets someone else into hot water.

. . .

Sadly, sometimes saboteurs can use the power of deflection for evil and make other people look bad on purpose. This is then categorized as a trait of a narcissist. Not only do they revel in pushing blame on others, but they also thrive on doing so because it strokes their ego. They take so much sadistic enjoyment out of hurting others in a bid to make themselves look good because they never want to be perceived as imperfect.

**8. Dislike for Your Current Reality.** Why do so many people watch smutty TV or play video games? Because you get to be in the controlling seat! Here, you can be a dominator, even though it is in a fictional world! It's a form of what is known as escapism, and because you have many options to rule the game and strategy, you choose to rather play video games as opposed to dealing with reality and its uncertain outcomes. It is directly translated to procrastination as a self-sabotaging tendency.

Procrastination is a serious problem amongst many saboteurs, especially the younger generations. There are many reasons why video games are correlated to procrastination, but in a study done amongst 500 participants, it was found that video games offer feedback and instant gratification and provide a distraction from the reality of tasks that are not as tempting or rewarding.

The study was divided into two sections on video gaming habits and to measure procrastination tendencies in gamers. The first study comprised the gamers performing what is known as experiential discounting tasks (putting off doing something temporarily and playing video games instead), and study two used the method of a five-day trial where the participants were discounting tasks (putting off doing something permanently to play video games instead). The study aimed to explore the gamers' preference for delaying in seeking more significant rewards.

The results in study one concluded that hours of playtime were not largely attributed to the discount rate or procrastination as a whole. Study two's results yielded the same outcome. However, when the gamers were asked why they play, the majority answered that they are escaping reality and reducing stress and were more prone to procrastination than the gamers playing for reward, social reasons, or entertainment. So the link between procrastination and gaming was positive, albeit slightly weak at $r(513) = 1.22$ (Norby et al., 2019).

## Darius's Story of Hope - Conquering Impostor Syndrome and the Ultimate Fight for Survival

*This is a true account of a genuine person - the name and personal details are changed to maintain anonymity. In his specific use case, he is battling with bouts of Impostor Syndrome, and this is his story. He was in the epic battle for his life... So buckle up because this is the kind of story that probably deserves a Hollywood movie!*

Darius, a.k.a Dee, is an avid music enthusiast. He is aware that self-sabotage can manifest in a conscious or unconscious form, and it implies that it can be a catalyst in destroying your hopes and dreams and place your goals of successfully completing projects in the parking lot indefinitely, or cost you the ultimate sacrifice of losing your life!

He has agreed to share his story with us so that others may know that they are not alone and there is light at the end of the tunnel.

**The Haunting Past.** Darius is one of seven children and was born and raised in the beautiful country of Spain, where he spent his adolescent years with his father. Darius' story started when he was diagnosed with clinical depression at the tender age of eight. But, unfortunately, taking care of one's mental health and well-being was not a trend in those years, and the word depression was even more taboo as it was an uncomfortable topic for most.

The root cause of Dee's mental decline was due to an extremely hurtful childhood and pre-adolescent memories with the highest degree of pain imaginable! Darius' mother left when he was only six years old and completely vanished off the face of the earth, and he didn't know where she was. To make matters worse, Dee suffered physical, psychological, and mental abuse at the hands of his father.

As if this was not enough to deal with, he also faced bullying and racism in school. All of these events at school, which intensified with what happened at home, led him to hate himself because he was looked upon differently because of his skin color and facial features. And yet there is more! Darius also started to feel that he might actually like boys; sadly, this just escalated the bullying at school.

**Attempting the Unthinkable.** Darius has shared with us his tale of attempting to commit suicide–numerous times. The very first time came at the shockingly young age of just ten. Sadly, it would only be the first of many attempts in Dee's case. Most of the time, life became too much for Darius, and he tried to strangle himself. Out of all the times, the very last attempt is the one that is still firmly imprinted into Dee's head. He swallowed a handful of pills, and as fate would have it, the only effect it had was to give Darius a massive headache! This all happened before Dee's siblings were born, and with the new additions to the family–Darius stopped attempting to commit the unthinkable.

He never wanted his brothers to feel alone like he did and struggle through life on their own in their family dynamics. Eventually, he realized that he no longer had the motivation to attempt suicide–because he wasn't alone anymore!

When he turned 18, Dee decided that he had enough and immigrated to Scotland to be closer to two of his brothers and also started the trek to pursue an education in the Applied Science field. He simply decided enough was enough!

. . .

**Student Life Troubles.** Dee started his new life staying with his stepmother in Edinburgh. He enrolled in the Applied Science course, but in his first year, he soon realized that his full academic potential was not being put to full use as he found the level of course work to be too low and too easy and knew that he was smarter and could do more. As a result, this saw him dropping out. Another interesting phenomenon is quitting when we do not feel challenged enough!

Two months after arriving, Dee had the first big blowout with his stepmother. It got so bad that she kicked him out of the house. At the time, he fell into despair, thinking that the future had a very bleak outlook. While all this happened, Darius would spend his days daydreaming and reading by himself in his room. He would fantasize and conjure up idealist dreams of how things could be different and how he craved to experience unconditional love and would create fantasy worlds where he would have super-powers—basically all scenarios where he would be someone different—a magical creature of sorts with POWER!

After taking a break, he reapplied for the Applied Science course, only this time, he applied to the level that he felt matched his intellect level. However, even after doing so, Darius realized that science was not actually the field he wanted to pursue, and again, he dropped out.

You see, Dee's actual first love and passion has always been music. As a result, he applied for a course, but due to his ongoing what by now had manifested into depression, saw him drop out of school for the third time. At that time, this depression was at a dangerous level, where it consumed him and affected him more than it had previously. It was hard for him to do, but he realized that he had to take care of his overall well-being first as this needed to take center stage.

He took a sabbatical for a year, and in 2020, Dee re-enrolled in the music course that he had started previously and successfully completed it.

**Diagnosis Drop Out.** Looking back retrospectively, Darius feels that the reasons for dropping out thrice from school were multifaceted.

Dropping out from the first two years where he attempted to study Science, he feels that this was due to losing the connection to himself and purely acting on the aspirations that his father had imprinted on him and not his own. As a result, by the time he reached Scotland, Dee didn't know who he was anymore. Make no mistake; it wasn't because Darius did not like Science; in fact, he loved it! But today, he prefers to do his own research for the fun of it and not because someone else is forcing him to! He can look at it objectively because he realized that Science was not a career he wanted to participate in for the rest of his life.

**Taking it Back.** When we take a peek through the kaleidoscope of Dee's past, he'd be the first to admit that the gap year he took before launching his musical endeavors was probably one of the best things he could do for himself. During this year, Darius could re-calibrate his focus by reconnecting with himself and asking himself what HE wants to do with his life.

Dee has always been self-aware, but he would always try to justify his self-sabotaging patterns with excuses in the past. He eventually concluded that whatever he decides to do with his life is his responsibility. Subsequently, he is the only one that can and should take ownership to drive it forward. This meant that he had to accept and let go of the fact that the past didn't matter, and how he was brought up didn't matter either anymore.

He also used to be a person that reacted instantly in an adverse way when he felt offended by another person, and this gap year allowed him to self-reflect and take charge of his shit.

Darius is at the point now where it feels weird to him that he is not feeling like crap all of the time because being depressed was such a big part of his life growing up. In the mental sense, Dee has had to put in a lot of hard work and effort to change this situation, but he still can't help but sometimes feel that he is not worthy and doesn't deserve a good life.

**The Eureka Moment.** Darius decided to indulge in some *herbs* one day while socializing with his friends and the world came tumbling down on his head like a ton of bricks. He suddenly felt a sense of deja vu for what felt like hours at a time. He found himself feeling that everything he did or thought he did and everything that had happened was something that had already occurred somewhere in a time before. On this day, the lightbulb moment came when it presented itself in the form of an existential crisis that was pretty harsh in nature.

Dee was experiencing ongoing panic attacks for a week straight, which caused him to create a life philosophy regarding how he wanted to live it. It would seem that so much has been bottled up and stashed behind mental walls that at this stage, those mental walls weren't holding anymore, and all that has been gathered throughout the years has started manifesting itself in the weirdest of ways. This implied that he craved to live the type of life where he would have no more regrets going forward and one that is so fulfilling that he would look forward to what the future might possibly have in store for him. On the flip side of the coin, Dee battled internal conflict where he was asking himself questions like *"what is the point of living when it feels like it has all been done before?"*. He felt like the decisions had already been made *for* him, and the manuscript to his life's story had already been written—never for the narrative, tone, and style to be changed—somehow, this felt forbidden!

His visions experienced during the hallucinogenic effects of cannabis were quite disturbing as the majority of the time, it would be about his own death. So the fact that he was receiving these omens, so to speak did not help much when he was already experiencing anxiety attacks and just accumulated the amount of stress that he was feeling.

. . .

He realized that getting where he wanted to be would mean changing everything that caused him to act adversely and anything that prevents him from acing his goals and getting the things he wants in life and feeling the way he wants to feel about himself and life overall. Similarly, Darius knew that he had to accept that challenging scenarios would come about again, and things wouldn't always go as he had hoped. He had to take accountability for what he was doing wrong and appreciate what he was doing right.

One thing he knew for sure was that if he was to live this life again, he wanted it to be worth it, and this exact realization brought about the change in his life to want to take the next steps forward to reconnect with himself again.

One of Darius's friends also recanted a story about how they used to go and watch Dee perform and how jaw-droppingly amazing his talent for singing and music was, although he didn't believe in himself, which puzzled his friends greatly. Even though his friends highlighted his beautiful talents to him—at the time, Dee was not ready to be receptive to the genuine compliments he had been given.

Fast forward two years later, and even though Darius has come a long way in terms of progress and learning how to fight his demons, he still experiences those visions from time to time. However, they have become very rare. It would almost seem like as his life is getting better, these hard to explain episodes are no longer triggered.

Darius also found a sense of comfort by discovering that he was not alone in his peculiar psychic abilities. To his joy, he found a whole community scattered across the world. One member of this community accidentally now works with Dee, and he was able to discuss his episodic visions with his college. He was amazed that she responded by saying that she had been experiencing them since the age of 12.

Darius has certain theories of why he is experiencing these voyeuristic moments and what caused them. He wasn't prepared to share them, but one thing he does admit is that the calling–the change came just at the right time!

Did these moments of clairvoya hurt him mentally? Sure as hell! For him, it was like making the conscious decision to sever a leg that was already metaphorically dying– already festering with gangrene-like bacteria, and one that he knew he had to cut off or *he* would die! It was simply something that he had to do... This brought about a certain change in Darius. One where he sought new purpose and meaning–and he found it and is now incredibly grateful for it!

**Triggers and Changes.** The changes that Darius has been noticing in his life were not something that he was used to. For example, he had been experiencing romantic and sexual advances from both males and females, which was something that he was not accustomed to. Coupled with the newly-experienced female attention, he was getting noticed by random people and receiving compliments. During these exchanges, Dee was interacting with people that saw how much good he had in him that another self-sabotaging tendency reared its head, this time in the form of Impostor Syndrome. Despite what the people would say to him, he simply could not see himself through their eyes and didn't see what they found *so* good about him. He went on to say that he is not sure to this day if this is something that he is doing consciously or unconsciously.

When asked how he feels when people compliment him, Dee responded by saying that it depends on his current state of mind and from whom it's coming. For example, when a stranger pays him a compliment, he feels that he cannot trust them because he doesn't know them yet, making him perceive the praise as fake. As a whole, Dee feels that today he knows himself and that he is not as reliant on receiving credit from other people.

**A Musical Smoke-screen.** Musically, Dee is also still self-sabotaging himself. He keeps on telling himself that he will start to make music and seek the services of a music producer when he quits smoking. Because he hasn't stopped smoking yet, he hasn't looked for a producer yet. He feels that if he is to seek a producer before nipping the bud, so to speak–he will be forced to stop smoking, as he responds well to a looming deadline that is in place.

. . .

Darius has tried twice over the last year to stop smoking, and every time he does so, he realizes that it will become more and more difficult as time goes by. When he attempts to break the habit, it feels like he needs to revert back to it because it's a stress crutch.

The fact is that when Darius decided to embark on this self-improvement journey, he felt petrified of the unknown and the changes that it would bring about. He was so used to not feeling good about himself and getting told you are not good enough that he didn't quite know how it would feel differently. It was such a big part of Dee's life for so long that he feared who he would be without the pain. He didn't know if that would be a person he'd like to be and if Darius 2.0 would be someone people would want to be around.

The biggest fear of all that brought about change resistance was that he was afraid of losing the creative genius that was engrained in old Darius's DNA. He felt this way because when he wrote music, it was always about the dark side of the old Darius—where he experienced pain. So, in essence, Dee used his music as a soothing mechanism where he could express and channel his most profound pain and despair into. But, he took the plunge nonetheless, and not only did he like the person he's become, others have noticed it, and his music has also transformed and evolved into manifesting messages of hope—hope for change and hope for the future!

. . .

**Today.** Dee has really come a long way, but having said that, even today, he still has trouble detaching himself from the old Darius because that Dee did serve a purpose earlier on in his life by shaping him into the man he is today.

Looking back retrospectively, Darius feels that the most significant thing he has managed to change about himself is taking regular self-inventory and looking in the mirror and saying to himself, *"I LOVE YOU."*

This was very much a foreign concept to him, as he never used to do this in the past, despite advice from the people who reached out to him that suggested that he had to learn to love himself. He always used to think that this was a bit narcissistic and straight-up *bullshit*. Dee felt like it was an impossible feat, because like, *"I am my own person, how can I love myself—it's impossible."* However, he later learned to come to terms with the fact that it's a form of self-care, doing what is best for *YOU* and showing self-compassion—even when he might be procrastinating.

His inner critic would start rambling off things like:

1. *"You should've done this a long time ago."*
2. *"Why are you taking so long to do this."*
3. *"You're going to end up a failure because you are not doing anything about achieving your goals."*

As soon as this happened, Darius stopped these thoughts dead in their tracks and told himself, *"Let's stop here - this is just a thought and not my reality."* He has come to terms with the fact that he's had a difficult life, he's lived it and earned his stripes, but that he has two choices going forward; either to get out of it or allow it to consume him. Of course, Darius didn't want to let his demons consume him. Instead, he knew he owed it to himself and that he had proved to himself that he was more than capable of dealing with it. He has since learned to be more at ease with who he is, his capabilities, and talents–this makes him feel good, it brings him joy, and he loves himself for it.

**The Twin Inner Narratives.** Dee has always had regular conversations with himself, and the tone can change based on the two inner narratives he possessed. Voice number one is the Darius that is insecure, that needs validation from others, and this voice tries its best but doesn't know how to. When this voice popped up in Dee's head, it somehow synchronized with his father's voice–one that is harsh, hurtful, and just overall abusive. Living with this voice in his head brought back memories of living with his dad.

Voice number one realized that he couldn't continue on this path of self-destruction for much longer because it hurt the true Darius and kept him stagnant in his life. He came to the realization that Darius needed to change, which meant voice number one needed to change. And the result? Enter voice number two.

· · ·

Voice number two is the Darius, who possesses the knowledge and knows what he needs to do to achieve his life goals. Voice number two is one of understanding and compassion–one that is more nurturing.

When Darius reconnected with himself, he lived in a melodic harmony by fusing the two different voices into a sequential string that makes beautiful music. So you see, these two sides of Dee can sit down, have an adult conversation, and then come to an agreement instead of acting on impulse. In essence, the two voices can be associated with emotional and logical thinking and how these two need to collaborate to make life a best-selling hit–a song if you will!

Dee feels that his father was somewhat of an extremist in that he probably meant well being harsh on him but might very well not've had the tools to relay the information differently. Darius wishes that he still had a relationship with his father, but he feels that his dad has become stagnant by remaining stuck in his ways, and as a result, has never learned to evolve mentally. To this day, his father will still blame Darius' stepmother for pitting the siblings against their father and saying things like the kids don't like their father due to her doing. But, having said that, Dee's father still expects the siblings to show him affection, unconditional love, and respect.

What this means for Darius in the future is that although he would like to have children of his own, he is terrified of making the same mistakes his father did. He is also afraid that he will mess up their lives as his past and his upbringing messed his life up. But in hindsight, he is not wholly opposed to the idea.

**The New Dee.** Does Darius believe in tracking his progress? No! Because he feels that if he were to track his progress, it would defeat the purpose. He wants change to be a completely organic and holistic transformation. This means having something like a checklist or accountability partner would deviate from the task. The reason for this is because Dee is still figuring out who future Darius wants to be. The only thing he does know is that he knows the type of Darius he *doesn't* want to be. He still experiences fleeting moments of his former self, but they do go away.

Darius has learned to become more outgoing, and the way he treats other people now has also changed dramatically. Previously, he never felt confident enough to approach strangers. Today, he can talk to new people and build his network, making him feel good about himself. He can go out somewhere and be utterly excited at the prospect of getting to interact with a stranger instead of staying home all of the time.

Similarly, Dee feels that people's perception of him has changed too. In the past, when new people got to meet Darius, they didn't have a very good perception of him. Now, the people he meets love the person they get to know. In a sense, this was weird to him because he used to mask his true self previously, and one day he simply decided to be himself and found people to be magnetized by his presence, and now wanting to spend more time with him. As a result, he is at peace with himself and has never felt freer.

His advice to his younger self would be to try your best, even though you might never fully get the gratification where you get to the point to say that it's enough–because you have these high expectations of yourself. But always try to aim for the moon, and no matter where you land, it will always be way further than where you would've gotten if you never tried at all.

You should try and aim as far as possible, but always with a realistic point of view because failure is a given. Of course, we all fumble, but at least when you aim high, you are guaranteed not to fall in the same spot where you departed from.

Dee has a new lease on life; he is part of the movement today that believes when something terrible happens to you, or if you've had a shitty life, you can either allow it to define you in a bad way by using that as an excuse to live your life in a way that you know is morally unethical–knowing that you are hurting people and yourself, or you can use it to fertilize the ground for a new you!

Darius loves the warm fuzzy feelings of regularly indulging in watching sunsets, allowing the feelings of contentment and joy to wash over him as he basks in the sunlight, and he is happy that his life didn't end all those years ago–and for that, he is immensely thankful!

## Awareness to Effective Solutions

Our brain has connected the dots the way it saw fit - sometimes, those ways are not in our best interest. The good news is that every bad habit learned—in this case, self-sabotage can be unlearned. So your departure point is to identify which self-sabotaging behaviors are relevant to your specific case and become self-aware of them.

Once you've discovered which self-destructive tendencies you are inclined to, then you can start taking action against them and draft a strategy to combat their adverse influence in your life.

Sometimes the reason/s behind our self-sabotage tendencies are deeply seeded. With this, I mean that we fight the change in some cases, so we first need to be open to the change before changing those tendencies. So let's take a deep dive into why we rebuke against the change we so desperately need and crave.

---

4

---

## Resisting Resistance

---

*"Resistance arises from within. It is self-generated and self-perpetu-ated. Resistance is the enemy within."* - (Pressfield, 2003)

Since we have already established that self-sabotage is a defense mechanism, it is about time we start finding some ways to deal with this firewall healthily. One of the key things that prevent us from simply "not doing it" is resistance. This chapter will discuss why our mind tries to always force us right back into the comfort zone and how to battle this resistance.

## Unpacking Resistance

We briefly touched on this earlier in the book - when we decide to change something about our lives, we suddenly feel very uncomfortable as soon as we start to apply these changes. Like forgetting your phone at home and being on edge all day. No real reason, just an out-of-comfort-zone uneasiness. Be warned that this resistance will be one of your most powerful enemies to face when the time comes to change things for the better.

Resistance to the new you is like standing in your own way - it can be categorized as a series of psychobehavioral tendencies and bad habits that stop us from excelling in life and reaching our goals. It is also a concept that hampers us from moving from our current lower state to a more fulfilling one. Therefore, it's crucial that we learn to overcome it as quickly and effectively as humanly possible. **The most undeniable characteristic of resistance is that it's universal and experienced by everyone, no matter who you are.**

It is imperative to note that no matter how successful you are in life, it is impossible to eliminate resistance from our daily lives entirely. Instead, we need to understand that our tolerance to resistance can and should change when we open our minds to the magical world of opportunity that lies just beyond the confined zone, called our comfort bubble. This can be achieved by cultivating a type of resilience against resistance.

No matter the type of resistance you are experiencing, it can quickly escalate into something extremely harmful if you are not armed to cope with it.

## The Protean Nature of Resistance

So why is resistance so hard to combat, and why is it particularly hard to overcome as a self-sabotaging tendency? This is due to nothing other than its protean nature, as mentioned earlier. Just to clarify - when something has a proteus-like nature, it implies that it assumes many different forms.

Not only does it have different familiars - much like the shape-shifting witches in Macbeth, it is also constantly changing to such an extent that we can barely keep up. One very destructive form of resistance is when we project what is known as our own internal resistance onto other individuals and/or situations.

This is where we pass the buck with a victim mentality and blame everything and everyone around us for our misery and mediocre approach to life. But, unfortunately, while we engage in this type of projecting, we will never resume responsibility or control over our lives again, giving resistance a dangerous power over us. (The Psychology of Self-Sabotage and Resistance, 2018). So let's take a deeper look into the types of resistance and why saboteurs are so apprehensive against them.

## The Five Forms of Change Resistance

There are five primary forms of change resistance, and they are:

1. Active change resistance
2. Attachment change resistance
3. Overload change resistance
4. Passive change resistance, and

5. Uncertainty change resistance

We can use the following real-life case examples of these types of saboteurs and why they engage in this type of change resistance.

**Active Change Resistance.** Meet Kevin. Kevin is very unhappy at work. After a meeting today, all the staff members were informed that there would be a change in management structure for their particular division.

After the meeting, Kevin and some of his colleagues decided to go out for lunch. During lunch, Kevin dominated the discussion by verbalizing his disapproval of the new management structure and was openly saying that he would be rebuking against the changes the management structure would be bringing, such as proposed overtime.

In Kevin's instance, he is overtly trying to highlight all the negative aspects of this change, and his colleagues will quickly catch on to his behavior. In this manner, Kevin is influencing his colleagues adversely by getting them to do the same.

He is also going out of his way to undermine the change by willingly admitting that he will not comply with certain perimeters the change will bring about and is directly challenging the change.

. . .

**What is Active Change Resistance?** Kevin's behavior can be classified as modeling a fight because he actively wants to fight against something he perceives as a possible threat. This so-called threat that he is feeling is something that he feels compelled to eradicate.

By acting out, Kevin probably feels that he will lose some control in his job environment or might feel that the expectancy of the changes is not fair towards him. On the other hand, Kevin might actually love his job and the current role that he is in, and the change might be affecting this, or it might pose a risk of taking something away from him that he holds dear.

Kevin knows that the change is imminent, and he knows he has two choices in the matter—welcome the change or look for another job. For saboteurs like Kevin, the changes in their behavior will become apparent when they realize that fighting the change is futile.

**Tools for Overcoming Active Change Resistance.** For you as a resistor to this change, it's imperative to gain a solid understanding by addressing the change and exploring the situation from the perspective of what exactly would be changing in your life.

It might very well be that the threat you are feeling is merely imagined, and therefore you would have to do your due diligence to ask questions, understand what the change would bring and mean to you, and then explore the options you have to deal with it effectively.

If another person brings on the change, you have to air your concerns with them so that you can gain a better perspective first before just reacting. If you can do this, both of you can search and find a solution to handle your grievances as a change resistor more calmly. After doing this, you will find that your "fight" response can be addressed constructively, and you will be able to resist the urge to do so again.

*Damien's tip: If you want to challenge someone on a new policy/change - make sure you fully understand why they perceive this change is needed. In the best-case scenario, you will come prepared with alternative ideas to achieve those goals without compromising the aspects you are worried about. You will then be perceived as a problem solver and innovator rather than a moaner who only sees problems.*

### *Exercises to Overcome Active Change Resistance:*

*ET-Squared (Helps in:* Creating awareness of your self-sabotage triggers as and when they occur.)

*Time Required:* 10 minutes

. . .

*Instructions:* When you feel sad, angry, disappointed, frustrated, or in any way negative, name that emotion in your mind or out loud. Go to a quiet spot with your journal in hand. Close your eyes and go back to the moment where you felt this negative emotion. What happened just before you started feeling this way? Write all these observations down and everything you can remember. Go back to the negative thought and try to place it into a type of self-sabotage trigger and write this down too. After you've written this down, reflect and look back at it regularly to gain a deeper understanding of why so that you can take the required evasive action against it.

*Clouds of Thought (Helps you to:* View negative thoughts as just that and not something you feel compelled to react to.)

*Time Required:* 10 minutes

*Instructions:* Find a quiet place and take a few deep breaths until you reach a meditative state. Quiet your mind and pay attention to your inhaling and exhaling. Pay attention to the feelings and thoughts that enter your mind and observe them, allowing them to come and go freely. Don't try to analyze them, react to them, fight them or judge yourself on them. Instead, be curious about them. Pretend that you are watching a play, and this is someone else's performance, and examine each thought individually. After a few moments, gently guide yourself out of this sense of awareness and back to reality. Count backward from five to one and gently let go of each "cloud of thought." Just like you aren't able to hitch a ride on a cloud and have no other option to let it go, similarly, you need to train your mind not to hold on to negative thoughts and react to triggers that bring about your self-sabotage tendencies.

**Attachment Change Resistance.** Meet Amanda. Amanda has been lucky in the fact that she has been able to work part-time from home, and her husband has been able to support her dreams of being a freelance writer for quite some time. This is her happy *status quo*, and she never wants it to change! She feels like she has achieved the balance she wanted, and now that she *owns* this lifestyle - she will never let go.

Last night at dinner, her husband informed her that their financial situation had now changed, and due to Covid, he would only now be receiving half of his salary going forward. He advised Amanda that she would have to start working full-time as a writer or seek a full-time position at a company where she receives a fixed income due to this uncontrolled change.

Needless to say, her husband's suggestion of her going back to working full time has not gone down well. She presented strong arguments in response to his request in an attempt to resist the change to try and convince her husband that it is not yet needed for her to work full-time again. She said things like they can *"buy cheaper groceries"* and *"cut down on other unneeded expenses."* Amanda found random articles like *"15 easy tips to save $600/month"* or *"Cut your living costs in half without changing your lifestyle"* on Facebook and sent them to her husband. She was seeking any evidence, regardless of how flimsy, that would support her case to *not* change the *status quo*.

She tried her best to contribute financially since receiving her husband's news, but it was in vain. Finally, she had to accept the fact that the writing was on the wall, and she had to make peace with the fact that she would have to go back to working full-time. In a bid to make slight changes— instead of embracing a significant change, she said that she would look for a job where she only has to work a full day for 2-3 days in the week.

Deep down, Amanda knows that a delay in her starting to work full time can have severe long-term effects on the wellbeing of her household. Yet, she still denies this under-standing and stalls just to try to prevent those changes from taking place.

*Why is Amanda acting/feeling this way? Why the need to fight this change?* People like Amanda will present *strong* arguments in their defense to mitigate the change or stances that will support their claims. This way, they can then try to convince others to see their way in a bid to avoid imminent change.

They might even go as far as to make this big issue appear smaller than it is to make it stay the same. Then, when they see that there really is no other way and the change has to happen, they will suggest minor changes in the hopes of a compromise being reached.

. . .

Amanda is aware this is not a productive thing to do, nor is it the solution to her problems, but she creates this self-sabotaging behavior against her own better judgment.

**What is Attachment Change Resistance?** These saboteurs have a very solid sense of ownership for everything that currently exists in their lives, and in most cases, they've forged strong emotional ties to it in the form of attachment. In some instances, they might even be the creators of these scenarios by attaching a certain value to them, or they have successfully used it in the past because it has made life easier.

When an individual is heavily infused into this existing process, they are caught in the web of what is known as anchoring bias (relying too much on the first information they find) or confirmation bias (interpreting, searching for, recalling, and favoring information in a way that supports their beliefs or values).

Because the human brain cannot hold two conflicting views simultaneously, it makes it hard for this saboteur to objectively see the need for change or react positively to any replacement process.

**Tools for Overcoming Attachment Change Resistance.** Surprisingly enough, these saboteurs are not the usual suspects when it comes to resisting change, and they might not be difficult on purpose. If the hardware of their minds is constructed to support the status quo, they truly believe in the existing process. This can make them "blind" and ignorant to what those around them might see in terms of change.

Effectively dealing with Attachment Change Resistance implies going back to the drawing board and looking through the lens with a fresh pair of eyes—as if you are doing it for the first time. You would have to condition your mind to loosen the grip of anchoring and confirmation bias by thinking of things differently from the get-go!

You would need to refocus your purpose, determine the needs, and take inventory of the current data and how that is different from your opinion in the past. This process will form the departure point to allow you to create a new picture.

Be mindful of the fact that your mind will go back to your previous perception during this time, but your goal is to create a new neural network by conditioning and training your mind towards the new solution. So keep your focus on the new data and reinforce the new wiring (information you've come about that made your mind more open and receptive to view the change in a different light).

### *Exercises to Overcome Attachment Change Resistance.*

. . .

*"Yes, I know, but..."* *(Helps in:* Identifying the difficulty in a situation and the benefits change can bring about if you let it.)

*Time Required:* 5 minutes

*Instructions:* Every time you note yourself wanting to give in to one (or more) of your self-sabotaging tendencies, replace this negative feeling with one of positivity. Think of a go-to sentence you can use. Your first response will always be yes (because you need to acknowledge how you are feeling), and then you replace the negative thought with something you can do about the imminent change or pay yourself a compliment instead.

*Label thoughts and feelings (Helps to:* Remind you that YOU are in control and not your thoughts and that you don't need to react to every one of them.)

*Time Required:* 1 minute

*Instructions:* Every time you feel a negative thought coming on, add the phrase "I am thinking that"...before the negative thought. For example: "I am thinking that...I will never find a better paying job". This way, you've actually separated yourself from the thought, and you will notice that the level of negative severity has dramatically decreased in the process.

. . .

Pay attention to the fact that every time you add the phrase *"I am thinking that…"* how it seems to transform your initial thought. You can even take it up a notch by adding a second step. So, your next step is to say, "I acknowledge that…". Now your thought becomes "I acknowledge…I am thinking that…I will never find a better paying job." This simplistic two-part exercise will reaffirm to you that you are in charge of your thoughts, you can recognize a negative feeling, and you can label it just as a thought and nothing more.

**Overload Change Resistance.** Meet Jennifer. Jennifer was informed at work today that she will have to work from home two days a week with immediate effect. The vast majority of her coworkers have accepted this change as something minor and not very significant. However, Jennifer felt that this was not a feasible solution for the other members of her team because she thought some team members were already not pulling their weight, meaning the other team members, such as Jennifer, would have to "pick up the slack."

She complained to her direct manager about this as she wanted it to be known. Jennifer believed that this change wouldn't work and wouldn't be fair to everyone. In turn, her manager felt that there were no actual merits to her argument as the quarterly figures showed otherwise.

*Why is Jennifer acting/feeling this way? Why the immediate cynicism without even testing it out?* Jennifer is failing to see how working from home on certain days can actually benefit her. Instead, she is "moaning" and complaining about a simple change (in company terms) that holds no real value and won't even impact her that much.

Saboteurs like Jennifer tend to push back against a simple or a small change without any real argument that is relevant to the actual change itself.

*What is Overload Change Resistance?* This probably has to be the most common occurrence in workplaces. On the one hand, change is entirely normal, but the amount of change that is currently happening is not as consistent anymore compared to the pre-COVID era when life was "normal."

In some instances, the pace at work can be intense, and one change brings about another, and in many cases, these changes happen without you even contributing to them. Add these concerns to an already overworked, stressed, and burnt-out person, and "just one more change" can be the last nail in the proverbial coffin that pushes them over the edge and throws the whole apple cart over.

**Tools for Overcoming Overload Change Resistance**. It's important for you to understand that most of the time –just like in Jennifer's case, the introduced change was not influenced by the other changes that are adding to her stress.

. . .

The root cause of your apprehensiveness to the particular change resistance proposition you are finding yourself in is that you have reached the peak of your attention resources. You probably don't have anything else to give to change—because frankly, "there's just been too much change." When you push back against change, it's a natural reaction to stop the information from entering your brain. The best way to deal with this is to focus on your daily activities and maintain a positive and open mind about them.

### Exercises to Overcome Overload Change Resistance

*Box Breathing (Helps to:* Calm you down, slow you down, and aids in relaxation simultaneously.)

*Time Required:* 1 minute

*Instructions:* Inhale for four seconds, hold your breath for four seconds, exhale for four seconds, hold before exhaling for four seconds. Repeat the sequence as many times as required until you feel calm and relaxed.

*Physical Manifestation of Emotions (Helps to: Make you feel in charge of your emotions and experience better control over circumstances.)*

*Time Required:* 10 minutes

. . .

*Instructions:* Write down each emotion that is causing you distress in your journal. Move down the list, tackling them one at a time. Take the first one, and think about it as you inhale and exhale deeply as you settle into a comfortable position. Next, dig deep by connecting with yourself and think of how that emotion will look. Once you see a picture, feel this manifestation leave your body and come to rest in front of you. Finally, use your five senses by asking yourself:

1. How does it sound?
2. Does it smell like anything?
3. How does it taste?
4. How does it feel?
5. What does it look like?

After you've analyzed this negative emotion, imagine you can hold it in your hands and have the ability to change its size, shape, color, and even be able to make the emotion smaller. Then push it flat in the palms of your hands until it's the size of a mustard seed. So yes, it's still there, but it's much smaller and more manageable now, right? Then put that mustard seed in your back pocket. You can take it out any time to serve as a reminder that you can take any large issue and reshape it to a smaller one to the point where you acknowledge that it's still there but that you are better armed to cope with it. Repeat the exercise when needed as often as you like.

. . .

**Passive Change Resistance.** Meet Jeff. His girlfriend informed him that she would have to take on a secondary job to meet financial ends. Naturally, Jeff doesn't like the potential impact this might have on their relationship. All he can think of is how she is now going to be too busy to spend enough time together, and they will now have to work around two schedules, etc. Multiple negative scenarios flash through Jeff's mind. Still, instead of talking to her about his feelings, he kept quiet to maintain peace in their relationship.

*What is Passive Change Resistance?* For Jeff, this is a threat response that triggers fear in his brain. There are four primary forms of fear in this instance, and they are:

- Fight
- Flight
- Freak-out
- Freeze

In this type of resistance, people will display a freeze or flight response to fear. This implies that they want to either move or hide away from the change, hoping that it will pass them by untouched.

In certain aspects and scenarios, Passive Change Resistance may incorporate forms of overload change resistance, but in the majority of the cases, it is more than that! The only sure thing is that the idea of change makes them feel uncomfortable. The reason is that they fear they cannot handle the situation due to lack of experience, or they've already formed an opinion in their minds that this change will not work in their favor.

### Tools for Overcoming Passive Change Resistance.
The fact is that if you are someone that stays quiet when something is bugging them, it appears as if you are accepting the matter, but in truth, you are struggling on the inside. This is because it might not be a real threat yet, but you conjure up imagined threats and scenarios in your head.

The best advice that I can give you here is to externalize your feelings, thoughts, and emotions because only once you've vocalized them and released them from your mind will you receive a more balanced and educated perspective. This can come in the form of having a face-to-face conversation with one person you trust or in a group therapy session. You have to explore this fear more objectively to be receptive to changing your perception thereof.

### Exercises to Overcome Passive Change Resistance

*Opposite Actions (Helps you to:* Downgrade the severity of the negative emotion to keep you from self-sabotaging)

*Time Required:* 10 minutes

. . .

*Instructions:* Think of a negative feeling and assign it a rate from 1-10 (1 being the lowest and 10 the highest). Next, think of one thing you can do that is the opposite of what you are feeling. For example, *"I am going to fail my test next week"* and replace it with *"I am going to do my best to pass the test."* After doing so, re-rate your initial feeling - you'd note that the severity would decrease. Repeat and do this as often as needed.

*Mood Boosters (Helps you to:* Decreased the severity of the negative emotion to keep you from self-sabotaging)

*Time Required:* Activity Dependant

*Instructions:* Rate your current mood and assign it a rating from 1-10 (1 being the lowest and 10 the highest). Next, pick an activity that brings you joy (suggestions to follow in the next chapter for activities that will boost your mood. Once you've completed this activity, rate your mood again. Improvement, right?

**Uncertainty Change Resistance.** Meet Pete. Pete was at the water cooler earlier that day and heard that their CEO had sadly passed on. Pete and his colleagues have been pouring over possible future scenarios about their job security being brought into question. As a result, they did not meet their specified sales targets for the day as they were worried about what possible changes could be made in the company and how that would impact them, without so much as a word from senior management.

. . .

*Why is Pete acting/feeling this way?* Pete and his colleagues are prime examples of saboteurs being fearful over something that has not even happened as yet because they are concocting possible worst-case scenarios in their heads that currently hold no truth to it. Therefore we can say that because they are unsure of what the future holds for them at the company, they resist the change due to the uncertainty this "change" might have for them. This type of resistance is often referred to as the fear of the unknown by the general public.

### What is Uncertainty Change Resistance?

Our brain's activity is heightened in the face of anything too uncertain for it to process. It is then caught deep in the throes of having to work overtime analyzing these scenarios to make sense of it all by reverting back to patterns of the "known." In the majority of the situations that bring about change, there are too many gaps for the brain to fill in the missing blanks, and in turn, this results in more rumination of the brain as it tries to fabricate possibilities. This way, you waste effort on time imagining things that may not even happen. Furthermore, your brain will fill the gaps by imaging the worst possible outcomes, which will make you resist the change.

### Tools for Overcoming Uncertainty Change Resistance.
The first thing you'd have to do here is not to promote uncertainty in your mind. This is incredibly hard to do because once it has manifested in your mind, you can't stop the brain from running away like a rollercoaster!

When the brain ruminates, there are no time constraints to it. It doesn't have working hours and can keep you from a good night's sleep, and you can become so consumed by "what ifs" that you are unable to focus on anything else— which means you are in essence sacrificing your daily productivity and your overall happiness in the process. When you can establish where the uncertainty gaps are, you can replace these "voids" and assumptions of your mind by focusing on the facts you know.

## *Exercises to Overcome Uncertainty Change Resistance*

*Phone a Friend (Helps you to:* Share your negative emotions with someone you trust that can offer a different viewpoint.)

*Time Required:* 10 minutes

*Instructions:* Phone or text a friend or a relative and tell them how you are feeling, why you are feeling this way, and what caused it. Ask their opinion about whether they think the same way you do or invite them to share a different viewpoint. Asking an outside party can help you discern between a self-sabotage trigger and just a negative thought pattern.

*Keep your values close (Helps you to:* Live by your values daily and reminds you to live a life of purpose.)

. . .

*Time Required:* 10 minutes

*Instructions:*

1. *Make* a list of your top ten values.
2. Assign them in numeric importance from 1-10.
3. Focus on your top three first.
4. Create a sensory reminder of each of them, such as a photograph for your wallet, a keychain for your car keys, or a scent marker.
5. Make a point of looking at these sensory reminders daily to remind you of your values and why you are here.

## Why do we Resist Change?

A prime example of the reason behind resisting resistance is due to us willingly (because we can't help it, or as a culmination of our own insecurities) or unwillingly (because we don't know better yet) projecting our shit and the way we feel onto other people and worst of all, those closest to us!

Enter the victim mentality, where we conveniently pass the blame onto others or scenarios and things in life that have happened. When we use our failures in life as excuses for accepting mediocrity, we are blinded towards the responsibility that only we have to take to change our circumstances.

. . .

In turn, we also walk about feeling like empty vessels because we cannot have any form of relationship with any meaning and value to it. This spreads across the board, from a friendship to an intimate relationship with your partner. It can also keep us from reaching all the goals we want to achieve in life, such as getting a promotion at work, looking for another job, or pursuing studies.

In addition to this, the other reason we resist change is as a result of fear. That knee-weakening, perspire-staining fear that rattles you to the core and strikes havoc in the heart of even the bravest. Fear has two essential components attached to it:

- Fearing to become that higher-being you so desperately crave, and
- Fear of reacting against something that poses a threat to us.

Responding to fear is an adverse trigger that comes naturally to humans and is, in fact, healthy! In the instance of becoming a higher-being, it is at the epicenter of living a fulfilled life. But only if we can respond positively to the changes this will bring in our lives.

It is said that the more we are afraid of doing something that will challenge us to the core, the more sure we can be that we actually need to do this thing that scares the shit out of us!

## Techniques to Combat Resistance and the Fear Being Felt

Effectively combating resistance is a constant work in progress and a challenge that will be laid at your feet for you to master *every. single. day*! The ability to withstand the storms and move with the opposing tides sets successful people apart from the rest of the pack.

And don't for one moment think that successful people are not faced with the same challenges as the rest of earth's population. The difference? They have learned how to stand up against them and resist resistance! So whatever comes on their path, they know how to steer clear of these distractions along the way.

So I challenge you to define your opinion of the impossible the next time you feel that you are just "unable to can," or the words "I can't" cross your mind! You have no excuse! The next time you say something is not possible, think about an addict. That does not exist in their vocabulary! They will do anything and everything to ensure the next fix.

Who doesn't like to try new things? Perhaps you want to push yourself to try another workout regime in the gym? Are you now rethinking your answer? Of course, you are! Why? Because your brain is hardwired this way as a human!

. . .

As we've already discovered, the area of our brain called the amygdala is what identifies change as a threat and then releases hormones that make you either fight or flight, and this is your body's way of protecting you against fear. So this is why when we are presented with an idea that our brain can't compute, we resist the change.

The good news is that this psychological equation can be remedied by focussing on three things:

1. Our **dissatisfaction** with the way things are now.
2. A positive **vision** of the future.
3. Strategic **steps** to make the positive vision become a reality

## Gleicher's Technique on How to Resist Resistance

In the 60s, the so-called formula for change was developed by one David Gleicher at the Arthur D. Little Consulting firm in Boston, Massachusetts. This incremental model was designed to evaluate the respective strengths that will likely bear the outcome of the change. Even though this was created as an organizational change model, you can still successfully apply this in your private life too!

There are two versions of the formula in existence. The first is Gleicher's original formula:

**C=A x B x D > X**

- **C = Change**
- **A= Status quo of dissatisfaction**
- **B = Desired clarity of mind**
- **D = Practical steps to the desired change**
- **X = Cost of the change request**

The upgraded version was released in the 80s by Kathie Dannemiller:

**C=D x V x F > R**

- **C=Change**
- **D= Status quo of dissatisfaction**
- **V = Vision of future possibilities**
- **F = First concrete steps to be taken in the right direction to establish if the result of the first three factors are greater than (R)**

**R= Resistance**

Although these two formulas are slightly different in their composition, they boil down to the same thing: change *is possible!* The second formula was an attempt to simplify the equation to make it relatable and easier to implement in today's modern society. When D, V, and F are multiplied, and if any of those factors are absent or classified as having a 0 (zero) value, the outcome is low or non-existent and, therefore, unable to overcome resistance.

To then have a favorable outcome (resisting change), you would have to employ strategic thinking and use influence to create a positive vision and successfully identify the steps that need to be taken in the right direction to resolve the puzzle. In order to do so, it is important that you accept and embrace the current dissatisfaction you are feeling towards the change (Pennington, 2018).

## How to Get Comfortably Uncomfortable!

The first step towards getting more comfortable within an uncomfortable situation is to build up resilience against it that will allow you to cope better. It all boils down to my 12-step change resistance blueprint.

## 12 Steps Toward Change Resistance Resilience

**Teach yourself to be more open and flexible.** You'd find that the very first thing you would have to teach yourself is how to embrace changes instead of rebuking them. Change is a natural occurrence in life, and it happens so frequently when we don't want that change to happen. When you can teach yourself how to be open and flexible, you can rewire your brain by going with the flow instead of trying to swim upstream by wanting to control it. When you can do this, you'd be surprised to learn the many benefits change does hold in the cards for you!

. . .

**Seek strength in your resistance.** It's entirely natural for any person to meet any type of change with some form of resistance, and it's entirely fine! Some individuals have natural abilities to stabilize themselves, recalibrate to reduce any possible risk factors, and protect what is working for them, while others again can drive the change, explore it and then experiment with it. If you are a saboteur that is inclined to resist change because you are worried about the risks involved, you'd be better armed by researching and planning that risk and deploying strategies that drive towards the change.

**Ask yourself the question of what is it exactly that you are resisting.** The way to then overcome it is to ask yourself, "*What am I resisting*"? It is here where you need to be very detailed and transparent with yourself. In the majority of the cases, what we rebuke against is divided into two sub-categories:

- What we can control
- What we can't control

Your focus should always be on what you can control (such as your resilience to change) and then push away what you can't control out of your mind—albeit at a gradual pace—it's still progress in the right direction.

**Realize that you don't fear change; you fear loss.** Change is a situational occurrence in life. Resistance manifests during the change transition. It can be seen as a psychological process of embracing what is ending, working your way through the unknown, and accepting what is possible with the new change. This can be done by strengthening your bond with others affected by the exact change, relying on your support network, reestablishing your own purpose in life, having compassion for yourself, and utilizing all your skills and strengths to get you through the process and to condition your mind to adapt better.

**Cultivate a mindset of learning.** Nothing on this earth remains the same forever, so change is inevitable, and that is one thing that will always be true! When you resist change, you are, in fact, resisting reality! You should stop overexerting yourself on fighting change and finding out how to incorporate it into your life and become friends with it. When a jockey falls off a horse, they just get up and try again. My advice is to declare your vision and see the learning curve every situation brings to you, and then adapt yourself and your mindset to it! And, ultimately–have fun with it!

**Learn what you can so you can handle change better in the future.** Fighting change is futile, and it's going to happen whether you fight against it or not. So you should strive to work with a mindset that says, "*the person of tomorrow is what you need to work on today*" mindset. Change allows you to be creative and to grow as an individual! You need to learn as much as you can today, so you are better armed for the change when it does occur.

. . .

**Take into account the advantages of change.** Resistance comes from fear, and for many saboteurs, fear is a result of imminent change. The fear can be caused by not knowing the outcome or resulting from a previously negative outcome to change. Saboteurs tend to use resistance as an invisible shield to protect themselves, but in truth, this limits their experiences and them as people. Instead of looking at the risks and limitations that the change will bring, try to look at the change as something that brings about your next opportunity.

**Find a coach or a mentor.** Being stuck in the past and living a life of change denial won't get you anywhere, and even the most successful people in life rely on coaches and mentors to get them through, so what is stopping you? Often, we are so quick to run away from change because we are creatures of habit and comfort. However, a coach or a mentor can give you a different perception that can act as a life raft by becoming an accountability partner who checks in on your progress and serves as a "voice of reason."

**Look at change management as soft skill to upgrade.** Our human nature commands in our minds that we don't like anything out of our control. Therefore, it's our natural inclination first to seek to understand what the change will bring about before we want to become willing participants. So the best way to replace this mindset is to enhance your capability to embrace change initiatives in all areas of our lives (especially in today's uncertain and declining economic climate) and to install this "upgrade" as a soft skill and champion change in the workplace and life's other facets.

**Make the conscious decision that change *does* serve you.** Our belief systems are based on thoughts and choices that we've cultivated. For example, if you tell yourself that change is something to fear, then it will be. However, if you start to choose to believe that change can purposefully serve you and change your perspective, you can successfully rewire your brain and mindset around it, and it won't seem so daunting and scary anymore.

**Accepting your resistance to change.** We should first appreciate and accept the fact that change resistance behavior is normal! This will make your mind more open to changing your negative beliefs and thoughts that change is harmful, and changing these self-limiting beliefs will go a long way to recovery.

**What would you do if you wanted change to work and have a positive outcome?** A compelling question to ask yourself when these doubts and adverse reactions to change occur is "what is causing this resistance?" and challenge yourself by asking what you would do differently if you actually wanted this change to work for you. Once you can do this, you have the power to change your perspective and forge a way that can make this change actually work for you!

# 5

# Taking Control of Your Demons

*"Confront the dark parts of yourself, and work to banish them with illumination and forgiveness. Your willingness to wrestle with your demons will cause your angels to sing."* - *August Wilson* (August Wilson Quotes, n.d.).

Finally, we get to the chapter promised in my book description—and that is how to deal with self-sabotage. It's pointless when someone just tells you there are problems and doesn't provide any solutions to them.

## Self-Sabotagers Explained

Self-saboteurs can be divided into three main categories:

1. The individuals who create self-fulfilling prophecies.
2. The ones that are inclined to remove positive things from their lives.

3. The persons that lower their own levels of self-esteem.

We can delve even deeper and discuss the three most common self-saboteurs from each of the three categories.

## 9 Types of Self-Saboteurs Unpacked and How to Overcome These Traits

***1. Self-fulfilling prophet.*** This auto-saboteur holds themselves back in life in a plethora of ways:

**The procrastinator.** This individual is repeatedly putting things off and waiting until the very last. Naturally, this causes them to waste time, and they believe that they can only get ahead by employing delaying tactics, but this never gets them anywhere. As a result, the procrastinator is rarely surprised by poor results.

**The overthinker.** This refers to the person who is always analyzing and overthinking the shit out of everything! This person lacks self-confidence and overfocuses on the negative. Even something very small is quickly being reshaped into something that has dire consequences of epic proportions.

**The ASSumer.** Here we have a person who constantly tries to predict the future and control the outcome by taking action before these prophecies have even come true. They will act beforehand, and this keeps them stuck in a rut. They can never prove themselves wrong, and similarly, they can never see opportunity, even if it is right in front of their eyes.

**The Telepath.** This saboteur also likes to make assumptions and, as a result, shoots themselves in the foot. The telepath always thinks, "I know what they are thinking. They think I am [*insert a negative comment about yourself*]." This is because their levels of self-esteem are so low that not only do they not think highly of themselves, they assume others think so too!

### *Overcoming this personality trait:*

When looking at the procrastinator, overthinker, assumer, or telepath, they have all got the power to make them and others believe something that is not necessarily even true.

Because they create non-existing prophecies that are self-fulfilling, they end up believing them because they don't grant themselves the opportunity to think and be proven otherwise.

The best line of defense against these four self-sabotagers is for them to respond with the opposite action pattern (discussed in the previous chapter). This implies the procrastinator, overthinker, assumer, or telepath could battle their troubles by doing the exact opposite of what their self-destructive behavior is telling them to do. It would mean giving themselves more facts and evidence to show precisely where their auto-sabotage behaviors are taking them and how to open their minds up to a different, more positive perspective of life in general.

*Damien's Tip: You can also try and train your mind to make a conscious effort to differentiate between thoughts and facts. For example, if you have a thought like, "Everyone thinks I suck as a leader," - take a piece of paper and write down all the evidence to support or to deny this statement. Remain impartial, and you will see that the situation is far from being as dire as your mind made it appear. How many people said you suck at it? Probably none! The thoughts in your head are just that - thoughts. Recognize that a thought is NOT a fact and that your mind is sometimes playing games with you.*

**2. Destroyers of all things positive.** Self-sabotage and self-destruction don't always imply avoiding things that will take you to where you want to be. In some cases, it can mean going out of your way to remove any semblance of positivity from your life, and they can also be subdivided into three types.

**The avoider.** This individual is deeply secured in their comfort zone bubble. And they won't engage in any activity or thought that would take them away from this false sense of security. Therefore they miss out on key moments in life that can sprout creativity, liberty, or opportunities that can completely transform their lives. Nothing they do will bring them any feelings of joy and personal fulfillment.

**The protector of self.** This person constantly has an invisible protective force field around them, meaning their guard is up constantly because they feel a threat of imminent attack at any moment. The result? Never-ending feelings of loneliness and despair because no matter how many relationships they are engaged in, none have meaning.

**The A-type personality.** These control freaks are never caught off guard or even the least surprised. In doing so, they always feel in control at all times. Consequently, they will avoid situations where they don't feel in control at all costs. This brings about feelings of constant anxiety and a tendency to avoid social engagements and social opportunities.

### *Overcoming this personality:*

The crux of the matter is that these saboteurs live their lives in fear. They can try to overcome this so-called fear by employing what is referred to as systematic desensitization. It is a cycle where they expose themselves to these situations that make them fearful in a bid to reduce their response to fear. Overcoming this implies that you need to triage these fears starting with the least scary situation to the one that shakes your core the most. Start with the smallest fear and work through it. Once you have overcome that one, progress in your own time until you've banished all forms of fear from your life.

### 3. Self-esteem assassin

Enter the last three saboteurs!

**The overindulger.** This self-sabotager doesn't know what it means to achieve balance and moderation. They either have an extreme high or an extreme low - there is no in-between. Life through their lens means that it is either black or white. They can't ace their ideals because they lack self-control and, in essence, create a cycle of all-or-nothing, which results in a self-destruction loop.

**The self-critic.** This person is constantly putting themselves down by placing their life in a constant negative lens. Even if proof of anything positive stares them in the face, they tend to ignore it and will look for any flaw or damage within that positive prism. As a result, they have low self-esteem and are disengaged from wanting anything better for themselves.

**The perfectionist.** This individual has an impossible outlook on life and one that is very unrealistic. They've set themselves to an overachiever standard in everything that they do. This also transcends to others as they will hold them to that high standard too!

## *Overcoming this personality:*

These saboteurs all have a low level of self-worth. Thinking like them can lower your self-esteem and form a breeding ground for negativity daily. The way forward is to rebuild your confidence. Make a list of everything you are good at, look at that list daily, and praise yourself for your efforts. It would be best to focus on the things you did well that day and those that make you proud of yourself and your accomplishments.

## How to Change Self-Sabotaging Behavior

Sabotaging yourself is not an innate character trait, and it also doesn't define who you are as a person, nor does it take away your talents and strengths. However, it's possible to substitute auto-sabotage with self-advancement. You only need to start employing simplistic changes. Then, you progress to incrementally add more self-advancement methods until that bastard called your inner critic no longer has the power and the authority to hold you back! Here's how:

**Power up your level of self-awareness.** Start by spending time in quiet self-reflection to expand your level of awareness when it comes to your self-sabotaging tendencies. My best advice is to invest in a journal to document your thoughts and behaviors regarding self-sabotage. You need to establish where these tendencies are coming from. Stop multiple times during the day and have a self-check moment. The more you spend time developing insight about yourself and reconnecting with your inner being, the more apparent the path will become that you'd need to take to action changes. You will not need to do this forever - this method is mostly there to help you gain self-awareness.

### How does it translate to daily actions?

Try the following daily activities to boost your self-awareness levels:

- First, look at yourself objectively - meaning both faults and things you do well.
- Make regular entries in your journal to document your feelings, thoughts, challenges, and your joys daily.
- List your goals, priorities, and plans - break the larger goals into small, achievable pieces and smash them one by one, starting with the smallest goal first, which will power you to carry on with the larger ones.
- Take time to self-reflect each day - this can be writing about your day in your journal, talking to a friend, or meditating.
- Find an activity that helps center your thoughts, such as yoga - During this session, ask yourself questions such as, "What is my goal?" What am

I doing that is working?" What is not working?,"
"How can I improve on what I'm doing?".

- Talk to a friend or relative about your day.
- Take personality and psychometric tests to gain a deeper understanding of self.
- Ask your direct line manager at work for constructive feedback.

**Think before you react.** When your self-sabotaging tendencies make the rounds, you need to ask yourself whether these thoughts, feelings, and behaviors are hurting or helping you. So many times, we feel pressured to do something or will altogether avoid it because we are afraid. Taking a moment to decide whether your behaviors will keep you stagnant or propel you forward can go a long way in preventing self-sabotage.

### *How does it translate to daily actions?*

The Acronym T.H.I.N.K before you react translates into:

T - Is it TRUE?
   H - Is it HELPFUL?
   I - Is it INSPIRING?
   N - Is it NECESSARY?
   K - Is it KIND?

. . .

**Set achievable goals and a plan to action them.** If you have realistic goals that have meaning, it can help you live a life of intent and purpose. If these goals are then paired with a workable action plan on achieving them, it will be bomb! You need to ask yourself what your values are when you set these goals. What is it that you want more of in your life? What will create a life of purpose and meaning to you? What makes you feel energized and alive? Once you've done this, you can take baby steps that will drive you forward towards that goal.

## How does it translate to daily actions?

Set daily goals for yourself that are SMART:

- S - Be SPECIFIC about what you want to achieve for the day.
- M - Can you track the progress and MEASURE the outcome thereof?
- A - How ATTAINABLE is the goal? Can you do it? Is it within your reach?
- R - How RELEVANT is your goal to your needs? Will you feel accomplished when you've aced it?
- T - How much TIME will you need to complete the goal successfully? Set a time limit and give yourself a deadline

Once you've written your goals down, use these five steps to ace them:

1. First, list only three to four goals per day.
2. Write your goals down the day before.
3. Give yourself some extra time during the day to make provision for unforeseen circumstances.
4. Use the resources and tools that you are most comfortable with - whatever they may be.
5. Finally, create a distraction-free environment to work on your goals.

**Make minor changes.** Any positive action will beat any self-defeating action any day. But this all comes back to transforming bad habits into good ones at an incremental pace. Start by listing all your self-sabotaging thoughts and behaviors when they pop up. Next, rank them in order from bad to worse. Then, pick them off one by one by giving yourself time to change by replacing that habit with a good one.

### *How does it translate to daily actions?*

- The moment you wake up, name one thing that you are grateful for.
- Don't check your phone first thing in the morning when you wake up.
- Spend 10 minutes each day just to yourself and

gradually build it up to one hour. This means not talking to anyone, whether you just spend quiet time reflecting or doing an activity you like by yourself, such as reading a book.
- Live in the moment each day.
- Be 10x involved in everything that you do.
- Learn to be happy every day for no reason.
- Avoid random data. For example, read Twitter instead of the news, so you read what you really want.
- Turn off notifications for social media apps and games off your mobile.
- Stop complaining.
- Pretend you don't know anything about a topic and strike a conversation about it with a random stranger or a colleague.

**Be kind to yourself.** Making friends with your inner critic is a key factor of underlying auto-sabotage. It's crucial to replace self-sabotage tendencies and thoughts of self-criticism with gentle nurturing thoughts. You need to learn to adopt an attitude of acceptance by acknowledging your emotions and accepting that your past mistakes are part of the human experience.

### *How does it translate to daily actions?*

- Forgive yourself for your daily mistakes or the goals you haven't managed to complete for the day.

- Take care of yourself by grooming regularly, eating healthy, getting some exercise, getting a good amount of sleep per night, and finding a stress-relieving activity.
- Respect yourself and stand by your decisions.
- Treat yourself to a little gift like a chocolate or a long soak in the tub.
- Speak the qualities you like about yourself out loud in front of the mirror.
- Stop trying to be perfect.
- Accept and believe in yourself.
- Give attention to your dreams.

**Know what your strengths are and embrace them.**
Each of us has been given strengths, and you need to identify, acknowledge and embrace yours. You need to reflect on your strengths, recognize what you are doing well, and the positive emotions you feel when you do something. Ask yourself when do you feel at your best? Tapping into these strengths only once a day will cultivate and nurture a more profound sense of self-love.

*How does it translate to daily actions (examples)?*

- Claim your power - recognize your strengths and build on them.
- Explore a wide variety of professional roles and experiences.
- Expand your worldview by reading about and

visiting different countries and regions and seeing how they do life.

- Add value outside of work - volunteer at an animal shelter.
- Write down your own life story, or record it for playback later.

**Become a mindfulness practitioner.** Living a life where you nurture and practice mindfulness implies that you are grounded and fully present in every moment—it holds the key to separating the past from the present and brings you back to reality. This way, you can decide how to respond to any adverse reaction or problematic person that comes your way.

### *How does it translate to daily actions?*

- Focus on one thing at a time and complete it.
- Slow down on what you do to take in the moment truly.
- Spend time in nature.
- Eat your meals away from your phone, computer, or TV. Instead, sit in silence or eat with a friend/partner or family member (even your dog is great!).

**Find a mental health therapist.** Therapy can gently guide you to gain a deeper understanding of yourself.

Qualified therapists are experts on strategies and tips for combatting self-sabotage. Seek out the services of a therapist with whom you are comfortable and take the necessary steps to transform your life and turn it around for the better.

There are many forms of therapy available, and some of them specifically target self-sabotage tendencies by identifying the behavior and how to get rid of them for good. Some of these therapies are:

1. Acceptance and commitment therapy
2. Behavioral and motivational therapy
3. Cognitive-behavioral therapy
4. Dialectical behavior therapy
5. Mindfulness therapy
6. Strength-based therapy

## Learn, Unlearn and Relearn

The modern times we live in today dictates that when we are not at ease with ourselves and where we are in life, we have to unlearn how we've done things up to now (because obviously, it hasn't worked up until now) and relearn new and healthier habits that serve a purpose today.

If we are to thrive in a world today where everything is run at breakneck speed, then we've got to adopt a learning mindset. It implies embracing the natural inclination to rebuke against anything that brings us discomfort by letting go of the "old" and making space for the "new."

. . .

In the words of futurist Alvin Toffler, "The illiterate of the 21st century will not be those who cannot read and write, but those who cannot learn, unlearn, and relearn." So we can safely say that in the 21st century, it is now more pressing to take care of learning, unlearning, and relearning than ever before!

Are you finding yourself at this moment wondering what exactly you've learned in the past needs to be unlearned? Then try one of my following approaches:

## Navigating through your mental maps

Are you continuously questioning and challenging your thoughts by letting others play on your assumptions and interrogating your thinking methods? Don't! You're giving them an exclusive invitation to play Devil's advocate. Instead, you need to unlearn bad habits and relearn healthier ones to allow you to make educated and informed decisions to empower you to withstand the storms of uncertainty that lie ahead.

*"Yes, Damien, this is great! But how do I do that?"* Firstly, stop assuming and really get to ask yourself questions like:

1. Do you need to unlearn how you lead, motivate and manage others at work?
2. Do you need to unlearn how you communicate with your partner or the opposite sex?

3. Do you need to unlearn your current study approach towards your degree?

**Ask, ask, ask.** We were born curious in this world, and with that came a certain openness towards learning. Sadly the worldwide educational system has failed us to a certain degree by making test scores instead of creativity or adaptability the metrics of success vs. failure!

What is even sadder is that we weren't taught from a young age that learning doesn't stop in school. No, it's an ever-evolving project of self that is required for us to flourish in life. This is how we become better people, open the doors of possibility and opportunity, and improve the *status quo*.

The amount of learning that we do is determined by the number of questions that we ask. Right now, you are probably living with questions you've not thought of yet, or are too afraid to ask. As already discussed, our natural wiring dictates that we are susceptible to confirmation bias. How do we change that? By seeking out data that challenges and refutes our assumptions.

**Humble thyself!** Have you ever met a self-serving person? And by that, I mean someone too clever for their own good–literally! Of course, you have! Yet, did you know that IQ (Intelligence Quotient) is not the only factor determining success? You need to have EQ (Emotional Quotient), too–more on this later in the chapter.

. . .

In essence, you will only be able to seek out viable solutions when you can learn to become brave enough to acknowledge that you don't monopolize information. At the same time, be humble and receptive towards listening to the perspective of others that can broaden your horizons and viewpoints. Outstanding leadership requires a certain degree of humility—just ask former Presidents Bush and Eisenhower—let's face it, you don't want to be the only person in the room.

People that constantly walk around thinking they are smarter than the rest walk around with tunnel vision, utterly oblivious to their own faults and not receptive to the ideas of others.

**Go back in time and chat to the future YOU!** Think of an uncomfortable situation you are facing, but pretend you are facing it for the first time—ever. Then, imagine you have a portal or a time machine and go back to the past (much like Back to the Future). Now, look thirty years on in time to your future self. How do you see things differently?

Sounds crazy, right? But I can promise you in ten (never mind thirty) years, you will look back at this situation that has brought you discomfort, and with a more open mind, you will see how stuck you were in your ways then, and how this hampered your growth as a person.

. . .

**Comfortable with being uncomfortable.** As we've discovered earlier in the book, change will rarely bring about something that we are instantly comfortable with. Being of the mindset that "this is how things have always been" is no excuse to remain stuck in your comfort bubble until infinity.

Think about it this way; it's less taxing from an emotional perspective in the short term when you can learn to even just clumsily and slowly take the baby steps towards self-improvement. Copy+Paste might've gotten you where you are, but it won't hold much merit further down the line and will keep you stuck.

Sticking with the same routines and habits that essentially got you to where you are now (obviously a place you don't want to be anymore) will definitely "keep you safe," but in a world that is rapidly evolving, you will get left behind.

When you cultivate and nurture a mindset of unlearning and relearning, you shouldn't view it as a means to an end. Instead, it's the end itself! It all starts with accepting your personal identity and then rebranding and rebuilding it to your liking!

## Accepting and Changing Your Identity

*"If you know the enemy and know yourself, in one hundred battles, no danger. If you know yourself but not the enemy, one victory for loss. If you know neither the enemy nor yourself, in every battle, certain defeat. "*- Academy of Ideas (2018).

. . .

What are our identities exactly? It's how we perceive and self-identify. Our identities are made up of things such as:

- Beliefs
- Personality, and
- Values

## 7 Ways to Self-Acceptance

Accepting yourself and where you are in life can be an overwhelming and challenging feat. Do you find yourself being more accepting of others than yourself? Then this is a sign that you are too harsh and need to be kinder to yourself. Check my advice below.

**Realign your focus on the good that you do.** Self-improvement in itself is a beneficial thing. However, it's equally vital that you identify and set your sights on your good personal qualities, as opposed to just focusing on the things you don't like about yourself. If you can maintain this positive outlook, you'd be in a much better position to accept yourself and attain your goals by knowing which talents to rope in to propel you towards achieving your dreams.

**Prevent negative thinking patterns.** Viewing yourself in a negative light can get out of hand really fast! Everyone goes through phases whereby they can be moody some-times and, as a result, harbor negative thinking. However, it's imperative that you banish such thoughts from your system and find a suitable alternative in the form of something positive. A great way of doing this is to replace negative thinking patterns with words of affirmation.

Affirmations are defined as a series of positive statements that confirm your good qualities and bring the best you forward. The only thing you need to do is to dig deep and believe in yourself. You can either create these affirmations yourself or use pre-recorded positive affirmations instead (you can find plenty on Youtube, Audible, etc.).

**Practice positive self-talk.** Tying in closely with self-affirmation is engaging in positive talks to and about yourself. Not only can it change the current perspective you have of yourself, but it will also aid you in changing negative thoughts into positive ones instead. Make it a daily habit of looking in the mirror before you start your day and compliment yourself on your looks, outfit, a goal you achieved the previous day, and just for everything you do right by yourself in general.

Changing a negative habit into a positive one takes between 18-254 days. So do it until it becomes part of your lifestyle and daily routine. (Raypole, 2020).

**Accept the fact that you aren't perfect - NO ONE IS!** Having imperfections means that you are human. So instead of wasting time mind-loitering things that you probably can't change and embrace and accept them. Do you want to make the best out of your life? Accept your imperfections. After all, you are perfectly imperfect, and that is beautiful!

**Forget what others think of your decision-making abilities.** You are not a cake, right? So forget about trying to make everyone around you happy! If you do so, you'll only learn the hard way that no matter how hard you try, there will always be someone that is not happy about your decisions. Not only that, you'll be tired, worn out, and unhappy with yourself.

You need to base your decisions according to your goals and priorities and have faith and confidence that you need to do what is right for you.

**Stop worrying!** Constantly worrying about anything and everything won't help or change the situation you are currently finding yourself in. Instead of wasting your time living a life of fear, do what you can change to improve your situation for good! If you can't do anything to change the situation, focus on improving elsewhere where you can.

**Accept that you've done the best you could.** Make a conscious effort to be proud of what you've accomplished and your hard-earned efforts towards improving yourself. Dispel negative thoughts at all costs. For example, tapping yourself over the knuckles for something you've done in the past, or if you don't accomplish a goal, you've set out for yourself. If you've done your best and still came up short, forgive yourself, let it go, and move on by trying harder next time or doing something differently to gain a different result.

## Subtly Changing Your Identity

If you aren't happy with yourself and you'd prefer a complete overhaul, then this could be a life-changing experience for you and might very well be just the "ass-kicking" you need. If you can do this, you'd have the power to change your life!

### Subtle changes= GIANT BENEFITS

Sure, it's going to take some dedicated effort on your part, but if you can shift from a negative to a positive frame of mind, you'll start noticing some of the benefits in store for you:

- You'll stop engaging in negative patterns of thought. Examples of this include avoiding people, constantly playing video games, or procrastinating.
- You'll cultivate healthy behavioral patterns for yourself, like going to the gym or studying in time for a test.
- You'll save a lot of mental energy that goes wasted otherwise, and you'll see your daily struggles start to fade away.
- You'll have the ability to change negative beliefs about yourself that have no place in

your life anymore. If it doesn't serve you—toss them!

- Cultivate a mindset that you can do anything you set your mind to.

**How to change your identity.** Now that you know some of the benefits of changing your identity, next, we'll unpack precisely how you can go about it.

*Do it deliberately.* Did you know you can unintentionally change who you are? But think about the last time you did something good on purpose—feels great, doesn't it? Doing something unconsciously never feels so good as opposed to doing it with intent and purpose. If you do something deliberately, you'll get where you want to be much quicker, and it will feel much more rewarding than wandering around and waiting for it to happen eventually.

*Ask yourself: "Who is it, and what is it that I want to become?"*

Whatever and whoever this is, write it down.

*Take the first steps toward your transformation.* Now that you've written your ideals down of the new you, it's time to take action towards getting there. Set reminders, write your progress in a journal, make a vision board—anything that will help you get to where you *need* and *want* to be—i.e., the new version of yourself!

. . .

*Embody your new version.* So, you're now at the phase where you are doing the actions that will get you to where you want to be—but now that "old friend"—your inner critic is making you think things like, "Maybe this is not for me." The best way to fight off these thoughts is to imagine you are already that improved version of yourself doing these things. Feel this new person, be this new person you want to be!

*Drive it home.* Literally, take one minute out of every day to pay homage to your progress. Appreciate how far you've come—even if it's just baby steps in the beginning. See the change already starting to develop in your mind's eye.

*Think about what the future you will do when you hit a speed bump.* Ready that again! I said "when" not "if." Things *will* still be out of your control sometimes. Don't think of any distractions as not being the person you want to be.

**The next steps.** Remind yourself:

1. I am worthy
2. I am good enough
3. I am compassionate
4. I am a good person
5. I will do better every day
6. I will get to where I want to be
7. I did make progress today

*Damien's tip: If you want to feel better about yourself or doubt whether you are a valued member of society, I have a great tip for you. Do something nice to someone anonymously - don't brag about it, don't tell the person or anyone else (you don't have to hide it, of course, if they figure it out, but be someone's guardian angel for a moment. It could be something as simple as leaving a box of donuts at work for everyone without saying who they are from. Only you will know, you will receive no credit for it, and that is the very reason why YOU will know you are a nice person even if someone thought of you otherwise.*

## What is the Human Experience?

The Human Experience can be defined as the realities of our existence. These realities come in forms such as:

- Emotional
- Mental
- Physical
- Spiritual

One reality that I would like to touch on is the mental aspect. So many of us battle the symptoms of mental illness, and as such, it can be categorized as a universal human experience since so many of us can relate to at least experiencing these symptoms once in our lifetime.

## Self-Sabotage - Mental Disorder or Human Experience?

So when is it human experience, and when is it a mental illness or disorder? There are many opinions of this, and different people will draw the line between the two in a different place. Mental health disorders or mental illness refer to a series of mental health conditions. In turn, these are disorders that have an adverse effect on your behavior, moods, and thoughts. Examples of mental illnesses are addictive behaviors, anxiety disorders, depression, eating disorders, and schizophrenia, to name a few.

It's only natural that all people have mental health concerns every now and then, but a mental health concern is escalated to a mental illness when the symptoms and signs associated with the behavior partners hamper you from functioning as a human being and result in high-stress levels.

Mental illness has the power to cause you great despair in all areas of your life. Luckily, in the majority of the cases, these conditions are manageable by means of therapy and/or medication.

There are many causes of mental disorders such as:

1. Brain chemistry
2. Environmental before birth
3. Inherited traits

No matter the cause, if you suspect that you have any symptoms or signs of a mental illness, it is advisable to seek professional help as soon as possible. In most cases, mental illnesses don't go away on their own, and if left untreated, they can become worse and cause significant damage. There is absolutely nothing shameful about looking after your wellbeing, so please do not feel like this is an awkward or uncomfortable topic/situation. You'd be surprised just how many people you know have used or are using professional therapists. For many, it is simply a part of self-growth.

## Signs of Mental Illness

The symptoms and signs associated with mental illness can present themselves in many forms. They can also affect behavior, emotions, and thoughts. Some examples include:

- Alcohol abuse
- Always feeling tired
- Constantly feeling down and/or sad
- Constant worrying
- Delusions
- Drastic changes in eating habits
- Drug abuse
- Excessive anger
- Lack of sleep/trouble sleeping
- Hallucinations
- Hostility
- Inability to concentrate of feeling confused
- Failure to understand people or situations

- Overwhelming feelings of guilt
- Paranoia
- Sex drive changes
- Suicidal thoughts
- Withdrawing from friends/family/activities
- Unable to manage stress
- Violence

Sometimes mental illnesses can display physical traits too, such as:

1. Back pain
2. Migraines/headaches
3. Stomach pain
4. Unexplained aches and pains

If you are experiencing some of the above-mentioned, you need to schedule a visit with a GP or other related medical professional. Mental illnesses rarely improve or go away on their own, and if left untreated, they can get worse and cause major problems. Just an open consultation could be a good start, and your doctor can tell you a little more about the options available to you.

There's no one size fits all solution. But if you do have a mental illness, controlling stress, building resilience, and boosting amour propre can help you manage these symptoms. I suggest taking the following steps:

. . .

**Look out for warning signs.** Work with a medical professional to understand and learn what is triggering these thoughts and behaviors. Develop an actionable plan to know what needs to be done when these signs and symptoms return. Contact your therapist or psychiatrist if you notice any changes in behavior, thoughts, or feelings. Consider appointing an accountability partner that can help you catch on to the warning lights.

**Go for regular checkups.** Because you don't feel ill, don't skip your annual checkups with your GP. You might have a new health issue that requires treatment or experience adverse effects due to medication use.

**Seek assistance when required.** Mental illness can be more challenging to treat if you wait until the last minute. A long-term maintenance treatment plan can prevent a systematic relapse.

**Practice self-care.** Getting enough sleep at night, eating healthy, and exercising regularly is crucial. The best you can do is to take up a regular schedule. If you have trouble sleeping, have dietary concerns, or have questions about physical activity, talk to your GP for advice and guidance.

## Working on Your Emotional Intelligence (EI)

**What is Emotional Intelligence?**
The key to increasing our EI lies in our ability to prac-

tice a certain level of self-awareness. Self-awareness is when we possess a conscious level of awareness regarding our feelings and internal state. This is our ability to own our shit by perceiving, using, understanding, and lastly, managing our emotions.

EI used to be previously categorized as a soft skill, but in today's modern society, it's more of a necessity these days due to the fast-paced demand of life as we know it. When we use self-awareness as a point of departure in creating a higher level of EI, we can successfully establish the foundation of personal and professional development. So how do you build, cultivate, nurture and sustain a more profound sense of self-awareness? Here's how:

**Determine what your blind spots are.** The more you can learn, identify and understand the signs that your level of self-awareness can do with some improvement, the more you'll be able to spring into action and notice what needs to be improved. Some of the most prevalent signs are procrastination, stagnation, dissatisfaction, unfulfillment, lack of motivation, constant indecision, or feeling constantly misunderstood by others.

When you can relearn to be decisive and proactive, you'll have the power to move to action. One of the very first places to start is in your daily work environment. Are you defensive in certain instances? Do you blame others? Do you constantly feel the need to justify your actions to others? Then take a breather between meetings and allow yourself some quiet time to reflect and relive those emotions and the behavior and feelings that caused you to feel this way.

**Explore and confront your current belief systems.**
In your bid to create a deeper level of self-awareness and EI, you should examine your way of relating to your peers and your self-relation manner. We all have certain beliefs deeply wired into our brain, and we also engage in inner dialogues that limit and sabotage our potential. A pivotal element to self-awareness lies in understanding these beliefs and relearning how to tackle them head-on.

Often, these beliefs are self-limiting and present themselves in groups. For example, you feel the need to bring your partner gifts regularly and that you have to work extra hard to please them for the relationship to flourish. Instead of challenging them, we tend to look for proof to support these limiting beliefs.

You need to challenge these assumptions and limiting beliefs in a compassionate, non-judgmental, calm, and thoughtful manner. When you can do this, you'll be able to bring that limiting belief into question, and l replace it with new thoughts of your own that serve a purpose.

**Recognize your needs.** Many saboteurs lack the fundamental understanding of what their core needs are. When you can invest the time to analyze and determine your individual needs, you can develop a profound sense of self-awareness in all facets of your life.

. . .

Factors that determine our motivation and engagement are autonomy, competence, and relatedness. As humans, we all have some type of need for these aforementioned things to be filled, albeit at varying degrees. When we can learn to spend the time to assess each element, we can understand where the voids are and fill them. For example, our relatedness refers to our sense of connection with others, and we might very well uncover that we need more quality interactions to establish a deeper connection.

**Schedule decompression time.** When you've determined where your blind spots are, the next step is to learn how to engage in behavioral modification. When you have so much going on around you, how can you effectively take your mind back to a place of self-control and self-awareness?

One of the successful ways in which I personally do this is to consciously self-regulate my breathing. With this technique, I can teach my mind and my body to recalibrate my emotional state and bring it back to the point of control.

**Reflect Daily.** Self-awareness is made up of a series of pillars. One of these all-important pillars is the ability to self-reflect. You can do this in many different ways, such as taking a mindful stroll or journaling–basically anything that can help quiet your mind enough for you to understand what exactly is happening.

. . .

Many saboteurs have not been taught to discuss or identify their feelings, but they are crucial towards practicing self-awareness. In addition, they help us to highlight irrational thoughts and inner narratives that can chip away at our confidence levels.

By making time for activities that champion mindfulness, we can be brought back to present moment awareness.

# Conclusion: Self-Sabotage to Self Acceptance

*"Ambition, I have come to believe, is the most primal and sacred fundament of our being. To feel ambition and to act upon it, is to embrace the unique calling of our souls. Not to act upon that ambition is to turn our backs on ourselves and on the reason for our existence."* - Academy of Ideas (2018).

Sometimes when **the calling** comes, we might not be ready, but it's in that exact moment that our true nature and character are tested. The best we can do is heed that calling and get outside of our comfort bubble, despite our self-sabotaging tendencies getting in the way of our happiness and joy.

It's hard to pinpoint the exact underlying cause/s of our self-sabotaging behavior. Still, we need to ask ourselves the hard questions of whether our behavioral patterns in the past and up to now have been stopping us from reaching our goals and living a life of purpose and fulfillment. Our tendencies as saboteurs can come in many different forms, from chronic lateness to having intimacy issues in relationships.

No matter the reasons and causes, we owe it to ourselves to work through the challenges and build up resilience against them before we are consumed by self-sabotage that transforms into complete self-destruction. Not addressing self-sabotaging behavior can have serious consequences such as mental health issues, depression, and anxiety.

There are two types of self-sabotage. Whether we consciously or unconsciously participate and allow this behavior to consume us, we must look out for any signs or symptoms associated with auto-sabotage and seek self-healing or self-healing alternative therapies where we can channel those negative behaviors into.

Due to our genetic makeup, thoughts and feelings of self-doubt will always manifest themselves to most people, but it's up to us to take negative habits and replace them with good ones instead. The good news is that there is always a positive outcome attached when you focus on self-improvement.

The after-tremors of self-sabotage can affect us in many different areas of our lives, such as our careers, relationships, and even study endeavors. We read the sad but hopeful story of Amukelani, who served as an example and beacon of hope that you can change what you don't like about yourself.

Our brains are like computers, and it takes a careful balance of installing the right software to change the hardware and constantly patch our minds against bugs to ensure that the system is functioning at an optimum level. Delving into some of the common reasons behind our self-sabotage behavior, we explore Darius's magical story of hope and everything he was and is still going through in his pursuit of self-acceptance and banishing his self-sabotage tendencies for good.

The key to coping with life's challenges is to work on our self-awareness. Once we become more self-aware and reconnect with ourselves, the path to effective solutions against life's tidal waves will become more apparent. That is all good and well, but sometimes it goes even deeper than that—meaning that we actually fight the change that needs to happen in our lives, because let's face it—very few people welcome and embrace change. This phenomenon is called change resistance.

Change resistance can come in many forms, and each type has its own set of perimeters and tools to overcome it. I shared a few techniques to shape your understanding of change resistance and why this is good. The most crucial part is that you need to realize that you will be caught in situations where you feel uncomfortable. Still, your key to survival is accepting this and getting comfortable with it simultaneously.

There are different types of saboteurs, and each has its own set of tools and techniques that can help you overcome them. The key takeaway is to power up and upskill by understanding how you got there and why, then unlearning the negative behaviors —as they no longer serve you to try to relearn new coping methods.

Don't be too harsh on yourself; self-sabotage can be more severe such as a mental illness that needs to be addressed accordingly. Mental health concerns are a universal issue that we all share at least once in our lives, but if you need to get help–then get help!

Don't think that self-sabotage is a character flaw; it's nothing more than a series of behavioral patterns that arises from negative fear-based beliefs that are hampering you from acing your goals in all areas of your life. Instead, learn to be patient with yourself and seek professional help when you become stuck. The life that you want is well within your reach.

Thank you for embarking on this journey with me! I trust that you've found my guidance helpful and that this can serve as a reminder that you are good enough and that you are an extraordinary human being–you only need to see your own worth first. I wish you nothing but the best of luck on your healing path.

I would love to hear your personal stories and your feedback if you'd be so kind as to leave your thoughts in the form of an Amazon review. Have a great day!

# References

*5 forms of change resistance.* (2018, January 22). Mind Gardener. http://www.mindgardener.-com/blog/2018/1/22/5-forms-of-change-resistance

*11 strategies to fight self-sabotage (that work in just a few minutes).* (2019, August 19). THE CHALKBOARD. https://thechalkboardmag.com/how-to-stop-self-sabotage

*12 ways to overcome your resistance to change.* (2017, December 11). Forbes. https://www.forbes.-com/sites/forbescoachescouncil/2017/12/11/12-ways-to-overcome-your-resistance-to-change/?sh=3449f0a95833

Academy of Ideas. (2018, December 6). *The psychology of self-sabotage and resistance.* YouTube. https://www.y-outube.com/watch?v=CPIsRwf5Mmc

*Anchoring Bias - Definition, overview and examples.* (2019). Corporate Finance Institute. https://corporatefinanceinsti-tute.com/resources/knowledge/trading-investing/anchor-ing-bias/

*August Wilson quotes.* (n.d.). BrainyQuote. https://www.brainyquote.com/quotes/au-gust_wilson_808555?src=t_demons

Batauta, L. (2020, September 4). *The subtle power of changing your identity.* Zen Habits. https://zenhabits.net/identity/

Casad, B. J. (2016). Confirmation bias | Definition, background, history, & facts. In *Encyclopædia Britannica.* https://www.britannica.com/science/confirmation-bias

*Changing habits.* (2019). THE LEARNING CENTER. https://learningcenter.unc.edu/tips-and-tools/changing-habits/

Chua, C. (2014, June 30). *13 bad habits you need to quit right away.* Lifehack. https://www.lifehack.org/articles/lifestyle/bad-habits-quit.html

Clear, J. (2018). *Habits guide: How to build good habits and break bad ones.* JAMES CLEAR. https://jamesclear.com/habits

*Comfort zone quotes (290 quotes).* (2011). Goodreads. https://www.goodreads.com/quotes/tag/comfort-zone

Hendriksen, E. (2018, March). *6 reasons why we self-sabotage.* THRIVE GLOBAL. https://thriveglobal.com/stories/6-reasons-why-we-self-sabotage/

*How to be more self aware: 8 tips to boost self-awareness.* (2021, August 31). Develop Good Habits. https://www.developgoodhabits.com/what-is-self-awareness/

Hubbard, J. (2021, August 10). *From self-sabotage to superpower: Harnessing emotion with self-awareness.* FM Magazine. https://www.fm-magazine.com/news/2021/aug/harness-emotion-with-self-awareness.html

Jacobson, S. (2014, May 8). *Help! Who am I? 7 signs that you suffer from an identity crisis.* HARLEY THERAPY Counselling Blog. https://www.harleytherapy.co.uk/counselling/who-am-i-identity-crisis.htm

Jodie. (2020, November 13). *Diagnosis: Are we medicalising human experience?* British Holistic Medical Association.

https://bhma.org/diagnosis-are-we-medicalising-human-experience/

Kim, J. (n.d.). *We all have "issues."* MIND JOURNAL. https://themindsjournal.com/we-all-have-issues/

Liggett, S. (n.d.). *How to stop self-sabotage | Quotes to live by, how to stay motivated, motivation.* Pinterest. https://za.pinterest.com/pin/95631192075022928/?autologin=true

*Maladaptive behavior: Causes, connection to anxiety, and treatment.* (n.d.). Healthline. https://www.healthline.com/health/maladaptive-behavior

MedCircle. (2021). How to transform self sabotage into self improvement. In *YouTube.* https://www.youtube.com/watch?v=wVWAUpfezIA

*Mental illness - Symptoms and causes.* (2019, June 8). MAYO CLINIC. https://www.mayoclinic.org/diseases-conditions/mental-illness/symptoms-causes/syc-20374968

Morgan, W. V. (2018, June 28). *The Science of Self Sabotage.* Medium. https://whitneyvmorgan.medium.com/the-science-of-self-sabotage-e1ff3e448570

Nordby, K., Løkken, R. A., & Pfuhl, G. (2019). Playing a video game is more than mere procrastination. *BMC Psychology,* 7(1). https://doi.org/10.1186/s40359-019-0309-9

Pennington, C. (2018, April 3). *People are hard-wired to resist change.* Emerson Human Capital Consulting. https://www.emersonhc.com/change-management/people-hard-wired-resist-change

*Pessimism associated with risk of death from coronary heart disease.* (2016). BMC. https://www.biomedcentral.com/about/press-centre/science-press-releases/17-11-16

Pietrangelo, A. (2020, July 21). *Self destructive behavior: What it is & why we do it.* Healthline. https://www.healthline.com/health/mental-health/self-destructive-behavior#outlook

Pressfield, S. (2003). *The War of Art*. Orion.

Psych2Go. (2020, October 11). *7 signs of self sabotage*. YouTube. https://www.youtube.com/watch?v=Tbrj9aNRxr4

Raypole, C. (2019, November 21). *Self-sabotage: 17 things to know*. Healthline. https://www.healthline.com/health/self-sabotage#overcoming-it

Raypole, C. (2020, March 30). *Here's why you can't break that bad habit*. Healthline. https://www.healthline.com/health/how-long-does-it-take-to-break-a-habit

Ryan, L. (2016, January 16). *Five habits of controlling people*. Forbes. https://www.forbes.com/sites/lizryan/2016/01/01/five-habits-of-controlling-people/?sh=bb317fe203ed

Sandford, K. (2014, April 3). *How to stop self-sabotage and learn to be positive again*. Lifehack. https://www.lifehack.org/articles/communication/stop-sabotaging-yourself-5-easy-steps.html

*Self destructive behavior*. (2020, August 18). THE TREATMENT SPECIALIST. https://thetreatmentspecialist.com/signs-of-self-destructive-behavior/

*Self destructive behavior: What it is & why we do it*. (2020, July 21). Healthline. https://www.healthline.com/health/mental-health/self-destructive-behavior#bottom-line

*Self-esteem, Self-worth, and self-love*. (2021). Brave Counselling and Wellness. https://brave-mo.com/self-esteem-%26-self-worth

*Self-Sabotage*. (n.d.). Psychology Today. https://www.psychologytoday.com/za/basics/self-sabotage

*Self-sabotage: Overcoming self-harming behavior*. (n.d.). MindTools. https://www.mindtools.com/pages/article/newTCS_95.htm

*Self-sabotage: Why you do it and how to stop for good.* (2020, June 7). NickWignall. https://nickwignall.com/self-sabotage/

*Self-sabotaging: Why we do it & 8 ways to stop.* (2021, September 23). CHOOSING Therapy. https://www.choosingtherapy.com/self-sabotaging/

Seti, C. (2021, April 15). *9 Types of Self-Sabotaging Behavior That Might Be Keeping You from Achieving Your Goals.* PureWow. https://www.purewow.com/wellness/self-sabotage

Sharpe, R. (2021, February 12). *25 good habits for a meaningful and balanced life.* Declutter the Mind. https://declutterthemind.com/blog/good-habits/

Sounds True. (2012, August 7). *Brené Brown - Worthiness.* YouTube. https://www.youtube.com/watch?v=BHHghr-HUGOI&t=49s

Spacey, J. (2018). *47 examples of the human experience.* Simplicable. https://simplicable.com/new/human-experience

Spring, S. (2019, January 7). *7 ways to accept yourself for who you are.* Live Your Life on Purpose. https://medium.com/live-your-life-on-purpose/7-ways-to-accept-yourself-for-who-you-are-835f5ef4ec50

*The psychology of self-sabotage and resistance.* (2018, December 6). ACADEMY of IDEAS. https://academyofideas.com/2018/12/psychology-of-self-sabotage-resistance/

Warrell, M. (2020, June 12). *Learn, unlearn & relearn: What got you here won't get you there.* Forbes. https://www.forbes.com/sites/margiewarrell/2020/06/12/learn-unlearn--relearn-what-got-you-here-wont-get-you-there/?sh=633a11cd20a6

Williams, W. (2018, January 29). *Breaking the link between low self-esteem and self-sabotage.* PsychCentral. https://psychcentral.com/blog/breaking-the-link-between-low-self-esteem-and-self-sabotage#1

Wilson, C. (2021, April 22). What is self-sabotage? How to help stop the vicious cycle. *PositivePsychology*. https://positivepsychology.com/self-sabotage/

Printed in Great Britain
by Amazon

75694278R00095